IMPACT OF CURRICULUM REFORMS IN EDUCATION

IMPACT OF CURRICULUM REFORMS IN EDUCATION

Editors
Sarita and Monika Tomar

ISHA BOOKS
DELHI-110 033

Impact of Curriculum Reforms in Education
(*Education*)

Rs. 740

ISBN: 81-8205-117-7

Published in 2004 in India by
Isha Books, D-43, Prithviraj Road,
Adarsh Nagar, Delhi-110 033

Laser Typesetting at : Shree Vaishnavi Creations, Delhi
Printed at : Chawla Offset Press, Delhi

Contents

Preface

The last decade has witnessed rapid changes in society, working life and technology. It has been marked by a sharp rise in unemployment, especially among young people. These trends demand education system to provide young people with the abilities needed to face up to an increasingly changing labour market. The need for efficiency and productivity has demanded not only economy and cost awareness but also employees with many skills appropriate for several fields.

The education system is becoming transformed in a uniform way in all parts of the world and that credit accumulation and transfer, as well as interdisciplinarity in teaching, characterise education faculties globally. The new curriculum reform set out the principle that children ought first to observe in an 'global' manner, without too much order or analysing. Their analytical faculties supposedly began to develop around the age of ten, which teachers could respond to with systematic instruction. In this way, the curriculum displayed a gradual schooling within the school.

The present volume describes the current trends in curriculum reforms and its impact on society. It will be a highly informative reference tool for academics, policy-makers, teachers and students.

Editor

1

Educational Reforms in Knowledge Age

Education empowers individuals to contribute to society, fulfill their personal talents, fulfill their civic responsibilities and to carry tradition forward. Though these broad, societal goals have not, in principle, changed, our cultural context most certainly has. Having entered the Knowledge Age, our response to each of these goals shifts dramatically and brand new sets of demands appear, challenging our entire education enterprise.

Increased worldwide mobility, immigration, intermarriage, growing economic opportunity and other factors have led to a truly multicultural society in the U.S. Though the traditional goals of education in our society remain the same in the Knowledge Age, the potential for reaching those goals, and for experiencing some stressful difficulties along the way, are both very high. Though there have been many ongoing efforts to cultivate these skills, they are still not yet recognized as priority education goals for all learners.

Knowledge workers need to be able to: define problems in complex, overlapping, ill-defined domains; use available tools and expertise, both human and electronic, for research and analysis; design promising solutions and courses of action; manage the implementations of these solutions; assess the results; and then continuously improve the solutions as conditions change.

Fluency with the design process, project management, quality management, and research methods will all be important, as well as understanding the specific content knowledge of the field involved, which will be changing dramatically and will have to be continuously refreshed "just-in-time." Online information databases, quick email access to experts, and Web-based courses are a few of the tools that will help support this "just-in-time" learning.

In an increasingly multicultural society, a growing global economy, a world of increasing technical specializations, and a flattened "network" organizational model, cross-cultural skills will become more and more valuable. Knowledge workers will need to be able to craft effective communications in a variety of media for a variety of audiences. Given the bewildering number of communication choices available - printed report, electronic document, magazine article, e-zine article, book, e-book, print ad, TV ad, Web ad, phone call, cell phone call, Internet phone call, voice mail, telemarketing, fax, pager, Web page, e-mail, snail mail, spreadsheet, simulation, database, multimedia presentation, slides, overheads, floppy disk, tape, video, CD, DVD, radio, TV, Web-TV, teleconferencing, virtual reality - workers will be perpetually faced with choosing the right medium for the right message for the right audience, and with the challenge of doing it all as effectively and efficiently as possible.

Everyone in the Knowledge Age will have to be able to go beyond basic computer literacy to a high level of digital fluency and comfort in using a variety of computer-based tools to accomplish the tasks of everyday life. Needless to say, those who master the knowledge tools of the Knowledge Age will be much more successful at school and at work than those who do not. In an age of "at will" employment and increasing temporary and contract work, knowledge workers will have to manage their own career paths and their own continuous learning of new skills.

Since most work will be highskilled, project-based work (as opposed to low-skill service work or factory linework), the ability to manage a progressive series of shifts from one project to the next and to quickly learn what is needed to be successful in each project, will all be essential to career survival and lifelong learning in the Knowledge Age.

Despite the challenges, there are a growing number of school programs and even whole schools where these new skills are being learned and where learners are being prepared for the knowledge work ahead. And fortunately, what we've recently learned about learning provides substantial support for the acquisition of these Knowledge Age skills. We have learned that context plays a very significant part in learning, that the environmental conditions for learning (objects, people, symbols, and their relationships) are much more influential than we've previously thought, and that the transfer of knowledge from one context to another is not often successful.

The demand for more "authentic" learning tasks that match real world conditions comes directly from these findings, as well as the desire to have rich learning environments that offer a wide variety of contextualized opportunities for discovery, inquiry, design, practice, instruction and constructive exploration. This approach coincides with the need to become proficient in solving real world problems and to exercise critical thinking-and-doing in the Knowledge Age.

Recent project-based and problem-based learning programs where learners define their own projects (with careful guidance) and set the criteria for which they will be evaluated (student-generated rubrics that reflect current standards) have shown just how much learning can happen when students genuinely care about their work (e.g., The Project-based Learning Network, at www.autodesk.com/foundation/pbl). This fully supports the Knowledge Age need to develop self-reliant and self-motivated learners and workers who have the persistence to creatively solve difficult problems and find answers to tough, complex questions.

A strong case has been made for the social aspects of learning and the importance of learning from communities of practice. This extends the value of learning in context, discussed above, to the social and cultural realms of group interaction, peer and mentor relations, group culture, and the environmental influences of tools, settings, and techniques. Again, this firmly supports the Knowledge Age need to use collaborative, community-based approaches to problem solving and to learn from a variety of communities of practice in the pursuit of lifelong learning.

So many of the behaviors beneficial for Industrial Age learning become their near opposites in the Knowledge Age. Where learning through facts, drill and practice, and rules and procedures was so adaptive in the Industrial

Age, now learning through projects and problems, inquiry and design, discovery and invention is more fitting for the times.

Though information and communications technologies are important catalysts for moving into Knowledge Age learning methods, we must always remember that it's the practice and the results, not the tools, that make a difference. We can (and do) add lots of high-tech hardware and software to our classrooms without changing our practice, and end up with "electronic horse saddles," no more effective (and most often less) than before in transporting our children into our high-speed Knowledge Age.

And last, but most importantly, this new paradigm for learning presents a tremendous challenge and opportunity to the professional development, both preservice and inservice, of our teachers. In many ways, it represents a redefinition of the teaching profession and the roles teachers play in the learning process. Though the need for nurturing, caring, compassion and cultivating the best in our children will always remain at the core of teaching, the new demands of the Knowledge Age bring a whole new set of learning principles and behaviors into practice.

We are facing an unprecedented shift to a new kind of learning environment. It seems that moving deck chairs and polishing the brass on the Industrial Age teaching "Titanic" will most likely not get us to our desired destination. But inventing new high-tech learning "lifeboats" looks like a difficult task too, especially when the learning gear may need to be upgraded every six months or so. There have been three predominant approaches to improving existing educational system: "top-down," "bottom-up" and "systemic-mixed mode". Each has brought some degree of success to the reform of certain aspects of education, with most of the recent efforts focused on applying the more difficult "systemic-mixed mode" approach.

A great deal of effort has been expended to create rigorous new standards and frameworks for all subject areas; to expand the use of tests and assessments of both learners and teachers; and to broaden the range of experimentation in creating incentive structures and structural changes to schooling. With almost 74 million students currently in K-16 U.S. classrooms, they continue to improve their existing educational system. But shouldn't we also consider supporting the rise of an alternative system, one that is more in tune with Knowledge Age needs and knowledge tools, and that is increasingly proving successful in business, science, medical and technology research, and other knowledge-based institutions?

The kinds of knowledge tools disposal are much more powerful than those available even three or four years ago. Learning also supports the very styles of learning that will be necessary for success in the Knowledge Age. These three Knowledge Age forces - the new demands for knowledge work skills, the new possibilities that our knowledge tools offer, and the support for new ways of learning from learning theory - are all converging on a new, alternative model of learning and education.

A wide assortment of "visceral" learning resources - well-stocked librarymuseum-lab-workshop-technology-art-construction spaces, multipurpose music-dance-theater-recreation spaces, and outdoor garden-farm-biologyecology spaces. Plenty of access to "virtual" resources - portable computing with local network connections to learning and reference tools, productivity applications and personal databases, and global access to Web-based information resources and conferencing tools.

A wide variety of "just-in-time" learning choices for students and teachers from Web-based reference databases, libraries and resource centers, online courses and online experts and mentors. Online, standards-based assessments and certifications of knowledge and skills mastery, including simulation exercises and electronic portfolio reviews by learning advisory teams that include students, teachers and community experts, as well as in-person reviews of hands-on performance in authentic tasks by both teachers and students.

These Knowledge Age learning centers will extend into the community, with apprenticeships, local service projects, storefront mini-businesses, neighborhood projects, etc., as well as into the home through telecommunications. And the community will extend back into the learning centers with active community participation in a wide variety of projects and programs. The "turn around" reform strategy is based on promoting three important enabling trends - increased competition in education and training, decreased educational costs from the use of educational technology, and the effective use of performance-based educational practices and measures.

Competition to traditional public schools is growing very rapidly. Charter schools, private schools, for-profit schools, outsourcing of learning services to both non-profit and for-profit educational service providers, and after school tutorial programs are all on the rise. There is a strong desire on the part of entrepreneurs and the venture capital community to "break into" the $500 billion K-16 education market that is mostly "locked up" in governmental and nonprofit programs.

Though the risks of increased competition are high and must be carefully contained - threats to equal access and equal opportunity, the possible loss of democratic community control, the blurring of marketing and learning under commercialization, etc. - the benefits of a well managed, balanced level of competition may in the long run far outweigh the risks. Some of these benefits include lowered costs and higher efficiencies; access to a much wider pool of dollars and management expertise from the for-profit community; the use of the entire community as a classroom and learning laboratory; after school, weekend, and summer learning programs; on campus health, social, and recreational programs and services; and wider learning choices for students.

As information and communications technology costs continue to plummet while technology performance soars (Moore's Law), and as we increasingly integrate these tools into our educational infrastructures and learning practices, administration costs should drop and efficiencies rise, more resources should be freed for classroom learning (currently a little over 50% of educational expenditures actually reach the classroom), and more effective learning practices with integrated technology use should occur.

This assumes, of course, that the increased competition outlined above will force schools and other educational service providers to continually transform their programs and practices to benefit from the gains in performance and the lower costs of technology. Just as performance-based approaches are revolutionizing business and industry total quality management, portfolio-based assessments of employees, and electronic performance support systems with online knowledge databases and quick access to experts and mentors - applying these practices to education will help focus change and reform toward the new model.

Much work will need to be done to adapt and develop these tools and techniques for education and learning, especially in the tracking of student performance toward meaningful standards and goals, and in the devising and monitoring of common performance and quality measures for all types of educational service providers.

U.S. public and private agencies, institutions and programs dedicated to improving education and training are facing a very perplexing situation. They must perform a very difficult and intricate reform "dance." They must combine top-down and bottom-up steps to more systemically improve the existing education system, while simultaneously executing "turn-around" moves to prepare for leaps to an alternative education model still in its early stages. And it is in this emerging alternative learning model that educational technologies will play an increasingly important supporting role.

Educational software companies are merging into a few giant "edutainment" mega-corporations which often abandon the more difficult high-investment, lower-profit "edu-" development efforts in favor of lower-investment, higher-profit "-tainment" titles. Large school-based education software developers like Computer Curriculum Corporation and Jostens Learning are struggling to develop new curriculum models as revenues from their large-scale, traditional drill-and-practice-style learning systems level off and start to fall.

The Web is starting to look more like the world's largest shopping mall than a global library, basing much of its revenue model on the same advertising strategy that has made so much of commercial radio and television of so little value to learning. Billions of dollars are being spent on connecting schools, libraries and homes to the ever-expanding information infrastructure, while comparatively little is being invested in the learning content and support that will actually appear on our computer screens once they're connected.

On the positive side, there are promising tools for learning being developed by educational researchers and developers, innovative uses of technology are appearing in many more learning settings each day, and the tools, environments and methods for creating learning products are continuing to improve.

Though there are many examples of multimedia CD-ROM encyclopedias covering vast areas of knowledge (like Encarta or the World Book Encyclopedia), there are still very few multimedia reference works targeted at specific subject matter areas that are available to everyone on the Web and that offer a structured gateway to other related Web resources. The style of the learning activities in this environment must be consistent with Knowledge Age needs. Learning materials must provide more authentic design challenges where learners can collaborate on creating solutions to problems they care about.

Problem solving leads to questions and the search for answers - learners then have a reason to use the informational resources available and a motivated context for learning. Multimedia stories and adventures can help keep the engagement level high, but these must be integral to the learning design and appropriate for the intended audience, not a thin marketing add-on. On-screen simulation activities and hands-on kits and construction materials must also be an integral part of the design so that there is a healthy balance between virtual interaction and visceral, real world activities.

Though this "inquiry through design" process can provide a highly motivating context for learning, there needs to be strong support for getting past the necessary frustrations and creative blocks that are natural parts of the design and inquiry processes. Knowledge Age learners need support in developing their design and construction skills, their inquiry and answer-finding strategies, their creative and critical thinking skills, their project management skills, and their personal management abilities, such as setting goals, assessing their own performance, staying motivated and managing their own learning process.

Good trainers, teachers, mentors, counselors and parents have been the traditional sources of this kind of support and will continue to be throughout the Knowledge Age. But more and more of this help can be delivered through Webbased tools and databases, as well as through electronic contact with members of the relevant communities of practice. We will need Knowledge Age tools for creating and sharing electronic portfolios of work on the Web, for enabling multimedia discussions and collaborations, for getting quick help when needed, and for supporting all the stages of problem solving, inquiry and design.

Programmes for Educational Reforms

Today, everywhere governments have been embarking on

substantial programs of reform in an attempt to develop more effective school systems and raise levels of student learning and achievement. In these policy initiatives an unfortunate paradox that inhibits them from realizing their aspirations. The community of educational change researchers and practitioners has finally begun to learn something about how ongoing improvement can be fostered and sustained in schools.

However, government policy on education has not taken adequate account of this knowledge about school development, with the result that an enormous potential source of synergy has been lost and student learning continues to lag behind its potential. In recent years schools have been subject to a barrage of legislation and policy in many countries that has meant changes in curriculum, assessment, governance and financing. The nature of reform varies across countries due to unique combinations of historical, cultural, institutional and political factors.

There have, however, been a number of common elements, especially in the Englishspeaking industrialized countries. A general strategy has been to centralize educational policy while at the same time decentralizing the responsibility for implementation. Governments have instituted more restrictive curriculum requirements, including increased emphasis on science, technology and so-called basic skills, such as literacy. Traditional subject divisions have been reinforced in many cases.

Governments have increased testing of students and have made the results public, and in some cases put in place extensive external inspection of schools. While governments have centralized curriculum and assessment, they have decentralized many decisions from intermediate bodies such as school districts or local authorities to individual schools, and have given parents an increased role in school governance, all of which has put new pressures on professional staff.

Governments have tried to introduce market elements to schooling through increasing the opportunity-or requirement-for parents to choose schools (or, in some cases, for schools to choose parents and students). In a number of countries the status of teachers and their organizations has been attacked directly through unilateral changes by governments to the status of unions or to collective bargaining arrangements.

It is an irony of quite breathtaking proportions that the dramatic increase in educational reform efforts in most Western countries during the past decade is having insufficient impact on levels of student achievement. Admittedly there are pockets of success, such as the claims made for the English National Literacy Strategy, but in general the failure of recent reforms to accelerate student achievement in line with policy objectives has been widely documented. Milbrey McLaughlin gave a clear indication of the pathology of central policy change a few years ago in her reanalysis of the extensive Rand Change Agent study originally conducted in the United States during the 1970s. According to her, "A general finding of the Change Agent study that has become almost a truism is that it is exceedingly difficult for policy to change practice, especially across levels of government.

Contrary to the one-to-one relationship assumed to exist between policy and practice, the Change Agent study demonstrated that the nature, amount, and pace of change at the local level was a product of local factors that were largely beyond the control of higher-level policymakers."

McLaughlin comes to the salutary conclusion that "policy cannot mandate what matters." There is now an increasingly strong research base to suggest that initiatives such as local management of schools, external inspection, organization development or teacher appraisal, only indirectly effect student performance. These variables are too far removed from the daily learning experiences of most students. Those variables that do correlate with higher levels of student achievement are psychological, instructional and home environments.

The clear implications for policy are that any strategy to promote student learning needs to give attention to engaging students and parents as active participants, and expanding the teaching and learning repertoires of teachers and students respectively. The key issue is that if classroom practice is to be affected then teachers' behaviors and practices, as well as their beliefs and understandings, need to be addressed. It is teachers' struggles to come to terms with the technical and psychological aspects of the change process that leads to 'implementation dip,' and explains the levels of resistance characteristically associated with school improvement efforts that focus on classroom change.

Policy formulation therefore has to be concerned with helping teachers through the change process. As the OECD International School Improvement Project demonstrated, it matters little how "good" the policy may be, unless it is implemented then there will not be any impact on outcomes. While many schools are pulling the 'levers' of curriculum and organization, the precise ways in which these changes impact upon learning are unclear and usually unaddressed. The implication for policy is to place far more emphasis on expanding the teaching repertoires of teachers.

Impact of Curriculum Teaching Programmes

Much recent centralized reform places great faith in the ability of curriculum guidelines to codify and ensure consistency of practice. Although this ensures a degree of uniformity in the curriculum diet of students, it is unlikely to raise standards of performance. The policy implication is that government should be actively encouraging the development, use and evaluation of curriculum and instructional models in a wide variety of curriculum areas.

These programs need to be comprehensive, specific, contain student and teacher materials, integrate curriculum content with explicit instructional strategies, have an implementation strategy built in and be proven to work. Most education reforms are insufficiently differentiated to allow schools to choose or adapt programs to fit their own particular situation. Some schools' performance is outstanding over a period of time, others less so. Innercity schools may face very different challenges than do rural or suburban schools. It is therefore sensible to assume that a strategy for moving a school from a low level of performance to average performance would be qualitatively different from a strategy designed to move a school from average to excellent performance.

A strategy that helps to keep a school at an excellent level of performance is likely to be different again. The policy implication is to develop a methodology for differential school improvement strategies. School improvement works best when a clear and practical focus for development is linked simultaneously to work on the internal conditions of the school. Although this focus on "enabling conditions" or "enhancing the school's capacity" for innovation and change draws on the implementation research, it is an idea that is still not well understood.

The policy implication is to emphasize the importance of the relationship between an external change and the school's internal condition, and their combined impact on the school's capacity for improvement. If we are to increase the skills of teachers then we need to rethink our approach to staff development. The increasing evidence about effective practice, which comes both from formal research and from educators' experience, plays far too small a role in policy and in school development. An important role for government lies in supporting the creation and dissemination of evidence, so that schools can learn from the efforts of others.

Instead of every school "re-inventing the wheel," governments should be developing, piloting, disseminating and evaluating curriculum and instructional programs that directly address in feasible ways the targets that schools are setting themselves. At the same time, schools need help to improve their own ability to gather and use data. Careful analysis of achievement data, both from external tests and internal evaluation, should be a key part of any school's efforts to improve. Educators are generally not well versed either in data collection or analysis.

In Britain, for example, target setting, testing and inspection are central elements of the policy context. Horizontal coordination would suggest that all of these be aligned to support instructional goals and strategies. Vertical coordination would mean that classrooms, schools and local authorities receive consistent messages about what is required for success. In this respect, the proliferation of educational agencies and actors in most systems may not be helpful. The building of local capacity is as important as a coherent national policy.

Key elements of building local capacity are often in existence but not well connected with each other or linked to a capacity building agenda. We need to support teachers, school leaders and parents in learning how to implement and use these and other practices effectively. We also need a closer connection between schoolimprovement work and initial teacher training, so that new teachers come to their work with at least some understanding of key improvement strategies and skills.

Building capacity and managing real change require skills that most administrators now only learn through practice and experience, if they learn them at all. These elements, as well as local research and dissemination, could be integrated in ways that are much more powerful than their current separate embodiments. Some new thinking about appropriate organizational forms and delivery modes could have powerful effects in building capacity for change in schools, and in creating the enabling conditions that allow positive change to take place and to become institutionalized.

Above all, governments should insist that schools be thoughtful in their approach to change and improvement, but not necessarily require that everyone do the same thing in the same way at the same time. The only way to get people to think is to create and support the expectation of thinking.

Media and Education

There are two major approaches to using media and technology in schools: students can learn "from" media and technology, and they can learn "with" media and technology. Learning "from" media and technology is often referred to in terms such as instructional television, computer-based instruction, or integrated learning systems.

Learning "with" technology, less widespread than the "from" approach, is referred to in terms such as cognitive tools and constructivist learning environments. Regardless of the approach, media and technology have been introduced into schools because it is believed that they can have positive effects on teaching and learning. Media has many definitions ranging from "a particular form of communication" as in "print versus video" to "the industry that provides news and entertainment" as in "the media."

Media is defined as "all means of communication, whatever its format". In this sense, media include symbol systems as diverse as print, graphics, animation, audio, and motion pictures. Similarly, technology has many definitions ranging from "the application of the scientific method to solve problems as in 'the technology of space exploration'" to "the things or processes which embody knowledge or craft within a culture as in 'the technology of writing'." With respect to education, media are the symbol systems that teachers and students use to represent knowledge; technologies are the tools that allow them to share their knowledge representations with others.

Unfortunately, it is common for practitioners and experts alike to confound the meanings of media and technology in education, and they are often used synonymously. With respect to technology, people want to know whether various new technologies are more effective for teaching and learning than more traditional classroom approaches, whether some technologies are more motivating than others, or at the very least, whether technologies can be used to increase access or reduce costs within education. In the USA, the Panel of Educational

Technology of the President's Committee of Advisors on Science and Technology included as one of its six major strategic recommendations that technology be used to "Ensure equitable, universal access". Another reason for the attention being paid to media and technology in education reflects commercial or corporate interests.

Although printed material continues to be "the dominant medium format" in schools, a recent Presidential report in the USA recommends that "at least five percent of all public K-12 educational spending in the United States. Similar investments are underway throughout the world, in both developed and developing countries. It is no wonder that global corporations such as AT&T and Sony are investing in large-scale educational technology initiatives. Still another reason for the focus on media and education stems from sharp disagreements about the value of media and technology in education.

Enthusiastic endorsements of new media and technologies in education are easy to find in news reports, political speeches, and other sources. Many of these proclamations seem overly-optimistic if not hyperbolic. The controversy in the popular press is echoed in the educational research literature. Research examining the effectiveness of media and technology in schools can be traced back almost eighty years, and yet many questions about the value and impact of these approaches remain unanswered. Today there are several major reasons for the widespread attention focused on media and technology in education today.

These reasons include: i) the importance of unresolved issues about educational media and technology to virtually all members of society, ii) the enormous financial investments being made in media and technology in education around the world, and iii) the often vehement disagreements that exist about the value and impact of media and technology in education that exist in both the popular press and the educational research literature. The foundation for the use of media and technology as "tutors" in schools is "educational communications," i.e., the deliberate and intentional act of communicating content to students with the assumption that they will learn something "from" these communications. In educational communications, information or knowledge is encoded visually or verbally in the symbol systems (media) that are enabled by various technologies.

For example, animation is a form of media that can be delivered to students via a variety of technologies such as the World Wide Web. Within a web-based science tutorial, an animation of the movement of the moon around the earth might be shown to students so that they can visualize and learn about the lunar phases. The instructional processes inherent in the "from" approach to using media and technology in schools usually can be reduced to a series of simple steps: i) exposing students to messages encoded in media and delivered by technology, ii) assuming that students perceive and encode these messages, iii) requiring a response to indicate that messages have been received, and iii) providing feedback as to the adequacy of the response. Interaction in the "from" approach, if present, is normally operationalized in terms of student input via the technology such as clicking a mouse button to indicate a response to a multiple-choice question, some form of answer judging, and feedback in the form of another message previously encoded in the media.

There is also no consistent evidence that television increases either hyperactivity or passivity in children.

Another popular belief is that television viewing is detrimental to the academic achievement of school-age children and teens. While some studies have reported a negative correlation between the amount of television viewing and scholastic performance, such statistics are susceptible to misinterpretations because of intervening variables such as intelligence and socioeconomic status.

There is insufficient support for the hypothesis that television viewing displaces academic activities such as reading or homework and thereby has a negative impact on school achievement. Undoubtedly, the most widespread belief about television is that it fosters violence and aggressive behaviors among children and adolescents. The preponderance of the quantitative research evidence indicates that viewing violence on television is moderately correlated with aggression in children and adolescents, but as with all such correlational research, the evidence for direct causality is weaker.

Alternative explanations for the reported correlations are possible, e.g., those children with a tendency toward aggression may be more likely to watch violent television programs. Despite the weak evidence for causality, both the public in general and many politicians have come to accept the conclusion that television violence has negative effects on youth. As a result, legislation has recently been passed in the USA to compel television networks to provide violence ratings for their programs and to require manufacturers to install electronic blocking devices in new TV sets. Similar laws are already in place in other countries.

Less publicized than hypotheses about the negative effects of television on cognitive development, scholastic achievement, and social behavior are research investigations into the positive effects of television viewing on factors such as interest, creativity, and imagination. In the past, the biggest barrier to the integration of television programs into the classroom was the fixed-time limitation of instructional broadcasts, but the wide-spread availability of video cassette recorders (VCRs) has provided teachers with the ease-of-use and flexibility they require.

Increasingly, television is coming into schools via cable and or satellite transmissions. The Star Schools Consortium in the USA is one of the largest such enterprises, providing scores of telecourses in thousands of schools across the nation. Most often, programs received via satellite dish or cable are recorded by media specialists or technology coordinators and subsequently made available for teachers when and how they choose.

Flexibility of scheduling and ease of access to equipment and programs are the biggest factors promoting classroom use of television. CNN, NBC, and other networks broadcast news into American classrooms, but Channel One is best known for the contracts it arranges with school districts whereby Whittle donates TV monitors and satellite receivers to schools in return for guaranteed viewing time each school day. Whittle recovers its costs from the fees it charges corporations for product advertisements aimed at the captive teen viewers.

Interestingly, what little research has been done indicates that students ignore the advertisements and that teachers are not integrating the news portions of the program into the curriculum. Historically, studies of the large-scale implementations of instructional television have shown mixed results. Three major forms of utilization have been investigated: 1) instances where the total instructional program is delivered via televised teachers, 2) instances where there is an integration of teacher-directed instruction with television programming, and 3) instances where television is used to supplement teacher-centered instruction, either for enrichment or remedial purposes. Some studies indicate that students in rural schools, where quality teachers were less likely to be available, benefited the most from televised instruction.

However, television has been rarely used to totally replace teachers in any country, and television is usually used in coordination with or to supplement the regular curriculum. A large-scale survey of teachers in the USA conducted in 1991 by the Corporation for Public Broadcasting indicated that "instructional television is a firmly established teaching tool that is positively regarded by classroom teachers and increasingly well-supported with equipment and programming". The teacher plays the major role in deciding what happens in the classroom, and as long as teachers experience difficulty in previewing videos, obtaining equipment, incorporating programs into the curriculum, and linking television programming to assessment activities, television viewing will continue to be relatively rare in classrooms.

Interactive instruction via personal computer is known by many names and acronyms such as computer-based instruction (CBI), integrated learning systems (ILS), and intelligent tutoring systems (ITS). The personal computer as a tutor or surrogate instructor has been the subject for much research and evaluation since its development in the late 1970s. Critics of computers as tutors have been around since their inception, and there are vocal opponents of computers in classrooms today. One irony underlying research on learning from computers is that while everyone recognizes the amazing improvements in the features and capabilities of personal computers that have occurred in the past 20 years, few people outside the research community acknowledge that the nature of computer-based learning has also undergone enormous change.

These programs were essentially automated forms of programmed instruction. They presented information to the student in small segments, required the student to make overt responses to the information as stimulus, and provided feedback to the student along with differential branching to other segments of instruction or to drill-and-practice routines. Although this basic behavioral model continues to dominate mainstream educational applications of computers such as integrated learning systems, interactivity in some of today's most innovative applications, such as constructivist learning environments, is based upon advances in cognitive psychology and constructivist pedagogy.

Meta-analyses of research examining the effectiveness of computers in schools have illuminated their advantages and limitations. Meta-analysis is a statistical procedure that allows researchers to synthesize the results of numerous research studies comparing different treatments by reducing the results to a common "effect size". Integrated learning systems (ILS) utilize computer networks to combine comprehensive educational "courseware" with centralized management tools. ILS are marketed by large commercial vendors such as Computer Curriculum Corporation (CCC) and Jostens Learning Corporation. There were approximately a dozen major ILS vendors in the early 1990s, although recent mergers indicate that a market shake-out is underway. ILS are complex systems that involve the use of specific hardware and software to address large portions of the standard school curriculum, especially in areas such as mathematics, reading, and language arts. Funding for the development of early versions of these systems came from government resources targeted for "at risk" students, and they are sometimes criticized as having too much "drill and kill" materials in them.

ILS are most effective for those students with either low or high aptitude for regular classroom instruction, but that the 40% of students in the middle range experience no improvement from ILS over regular classroom instruction. Despite the lack of evidence that ILS are as effective as the commercial interests behind them claim, they are quite likely to play an even larger role in classrooms in the foreseeable future.

Intelligent tutoring systems (ITS) promote these systems as "the most promising approach to delivering individualized instruction" Although much of the development of ITS has been done in the context of military and industrial training, there have been significant efforts to develop ITS for education, especially in challenging subjects such as algebra, calculus, and programming. For example, John Anderson is well known for his work building a geometry ITS. An evaluation of Anderson's geometry tutor in an urban school setting indicated that the system had both positive learning outcomes and encouraged more cooperative problem-solving among students. Unfortunately, despite a few positive evaluations in loosely controlled studies, few ITS have demonstrated the significant results promised by their developers.

ITS attracted much more attention, funding, and research a few years ago than they do today. One telling sign is that the Journal of Artificial Intelligence in Education recently changed its name to the Journal of

Interactive Learning Research. Even those who have been most involved in research and development targeted at producing "intelligent tutors" have begun to acknowledge the lack of impact they have had on mainstream education. A major factor contributing to the lack of success of ITS is that the technical difficulties inherent in building student models and facilitating human-like communications have been greatly underestimated by proponents of this approach. Cognitive tools, are unintelligent tools, relying on the learner to provide the intelligence, not the computer. This means that planning, decision-making, and self-regulation are the responsibility of the learner, not the technology.

Cognitive tools can serve as powerful catalysts for facilitating these higher order skills if they are used in ways that promote reflection, discussion, and collaborative problem-solving. The process of education is not a natural phenomenon of the kind that has sometimes rewarded scientific investigation. It is not one of the givens in our universe. It is man-made, designed to serve our needs. It is not governed by any natural laws.

In the broadest sense, cognitive tools refer to technologies, tangible or intangible, that enhance the cognitive powers of human beings during thinking, problem-solving, and learning. Something as complex as a mathematical formula or as simple as a grocery list can be regarded as a cognitive tool in the sense that each allows humans to "off-load" memorization or other mental tasks onto an external resource. Today, computer software programs are examples of exceptionally powerful cognitive tools.

Computers as cognitive tools represent quite a different approach from media and technology as vehicles for educational communications. Computer-based cognitive tools have been intentionally adapted or developed to function as intellectual partners to enable and facilitate critical thinking and higher order learning. In the cognitive tools approach, information is not encoded in predefined educational communications which are then used to transmit knowledge to students. Although there are many different types of computer-based cognitive tools, including databases, spreadsheets, semantic networks, expert systems, multimedia/hypermedia construction software, computer-based conferencing, collaborative knowledge construction environments, computer programming languages, microworlds, and interactive learning environments, multimedia construction software programs such as HyperStudio are tools increasingly available in K-12 schools, and therefore deserve special attention.

Multimedia is the integration of more than one medium into some form of communication or experience delivered via a computer. Most often, multimedia refers to the integration of media such as text, sound, graphics, animation, video, imaging, and spatial modeling into a computer system. Employing relatively inexpensive desktop computers, users are now able to capture sounds and video, manipulate audio and images to achieve special effects, synthesize audio and video, create sophisticated graphics including animation, and integrate them all into a single multimedia presentation. Individuals with very little experience are becoming their own multimedia artists, producers, and publishers.

Multimedia presentations are engaging because they are multimodal. In other words, multimedia can stimulate more than one sense at a time, and in doing so, may be more attention-getting and attention-holding. In the cognitive tools approach, multimedia is not a form of instruction to learn from, but rather a tool for constructing and learning with. Learners may create their own multimedia knowledge representations that reflect their own perspectives on or understanding of ideas.

For the cognitive scientists, learning theorists, instructional designers, and teachers involved in creating constructivist learning environments, learning refers to the development of mental states and abilities of all types including conceptual knowledge, technical skills, automatic rules, mental models, and problem-solving. Forms of higher-order outcomes such as motivation, intellectual curiosity, and the habits of lifelong learning are especially relevant because these are the most challenging types of learning to teach and learn.

In other words, the real power of media and technology to improve education may only be realized when students actively use them as cognitive tools rather than simply perceive and interact with them as tutors or repositories of information. At the same time, there is a paucity of empirical evidence that media and technology are any more effective than other instructional approaches. This is because most research studies confound media and methods. The search for unique learning effects from particular media and technologies is ultimately futile because fifty years of media and technology comparison studies indicate no significant differences in most instances.

Whatever differences are found can usually be explained by differences in instructional design, novelty effects, or other factors. However, even though media and technology may lack unique instructional effects, some educational objectives are more easily achieved with media and technology than in other ways. For example, certain symbol systems can only be experienced with specific technologies, e.g., slow motion is a medium afforded by film and video. A teacher could try to describe the flight of a bumble bee for hours without enabling students to perceive its mystery, whereas a slow motion video reveals the wonder of the bee's flight in seconds.

Media and technology have many other advantages in terms of repeatability, transportability, and increased equity of access. Media and technology can be more or less well-designed depending on the talents, resources, and timelines available for the development effort. There are numerous scientific principles to guide design, but every instructional development effort involves large amounts of creativity and hard work. There are no comprehensive or infallible instructional design formulas. In fact, the design of media and technology for education retains as many aspects of a craft as it does a science. Implementation at the local level is as important as instructional design.

Implementation of Educational Reforms

In the 1990s, education reform has emerged as a seemingly top-priority political issue in both developed and developing countries. Improving the quality of education has become associated with two highly cherished goals of modern states. First, improving the quality of education is increasingly seen as a source of international economic competitiveness of nations.

In a globalized economy, countries compete with one another for markets, foreign investment, technological development, and hosting of multinationals. A highly educated workforce is seeing as conferring a competitive edge in this economic competition. Since the 1970s, the mantra of education specialists has been that improving education is a necessary precondition for development. However, governments seldom listened. Instead, they treated education as nothing more than a social right or entitlement, which they provided to their citizens depending on the extent of their social commitment, fiscal resources, or inclination to use the educational system as a mechanism of political co-optation.

Today, this has changed. Rather than viewing education as a mere social obligation of the state, governments have begun to see it as a necessary catalyst for development. In 1993, the World Bank concluded that a crucial factor in the economic success of East Asia was investment in human capital, especially through well targeted educational investments. This conclusion is finally being taken seriously by many governments. In addition to this growing consensus on the link between education reform and the national interest of nations, the external pressure for education reform has reached a new high in the 1990s.

Multilateral lending institutions often recommend education reform as part of the package of economic and state reform. In Latin America, for instance, Puryear argues that a new constellation of external forces pushing for reform has emerged, including: the need to compete in a global economy; the availability of new ideas about the negative economic effects of inefficient education; and the emergence of new international actors such as development banks, bilateral aid agencies, international NGOs and consulting firms.

In the 1998 Summit of the Americas, which gathered all heads of governments of the Western Hemisphere, improving education emerged as the top agenda item. Finally, education has become a top priority for both the political right and political left in many countries. Advocates of market-economics concede that education remains a legitimate area for state action, promising to make labor markets more competitive. Advocates of state involvement in the economy value educational reform as well, because it is an area in which states can still prove their usefulness.

In sum, education reform is enjoying a new impetus in policy circles. The systemic pressure and the ideological consensus on the need for reform seems to have reached a new high in the 1990s. A useful starting point for studying the political difficulties associated with implementing education reform is through a cost-benefit analysis. Scholars argue that when the costs of a particular policy fall directly and intensely on specific interest groups, and its benefits are too diffuse, policy adoption is politically difficult.

For instance, imposing ever increasing safety standards on automobiles produces enormous concentrated costs on automobile makers. The benefits of this measure, however, are spread over many citizens and organizations. Consequently, the politics surrounding this policy option will feature an oversupply of veto groups and an undersupply of reform demanders. Education reforms can be analyzed using Wilson's matrix. Generally, there are two broad type of educational reforms: access reforms and quality reforms. Access reforms consist of increasing the availability of educational programs and opportunities. They normally include expansion of schools, teachers, enrollments, teaching supplies, etc. Quality reforms, on the other-hand, seek to improve the efficiency of invested resources, with the goal of improving the academic performance of students within reasonable investments.

Quality reforms normally entail maximizing teacher productivity, reducing student drop-out or repetition rates, achieving optimum teacher/student ratios, sanctioning underperformance of teachers, etc. In Wilson's matrix, access reforms would fall under policies that generate concentrated benefits and diffused costs, whereas quality reforms are the exact mirror image. Access reforms produce concentrated beneficiaries: enrolled students and parents, teachers and teachers' unions, construction builders, bureaucrats whose budgets increase. At the same time, their costs are spread across a wide group (tax payers). Quality reforms, on the other hand, generate diffused benefits and concentrated costs.

Society at large, and incumbent politicians draw some benefits (e.g., a more educated society), but this benefit will be too general, spread across a large number of actors, and mostly perceptible only in the long term. For this reason, beneficiaries are unlikely to turn into powerful demanders of reform. Latin America, do not tend be heavy users of primary and secondary education services, or at least not as much as they are users of tertiary education.

Whereas beneficiaries are unlikely to express their preferences forcefully, cost-bearers will create huge stirs. Education reforms are likely to give rise to activism on the part of those who bear their costs. Moreover, potential losers of education reforms are politically well suited to put up a fight against the reforms. Teachers' unions, for instance, tend to be highly centralized and well organized, which allows them to resolve collective action problems more easily. In addition, they often operate in a monopsony and thus a single contract, which gives teacher unions a strong magnetic power: teachers throughout the countries are more likely than workers in other sectors to a union.

In sum, Wilson's cost-benefit/interest group analysis point to several political problems. Quality reforms generate concentrated losers, who are likely to organize effectively to block the reforms. Governments simply do not face sufficient incentives to persevere with quality education reforms, or alternatively, they do not face high enough penalties for faltering on their commitment to quality reforms. To understand this, it is important to understand the differences in incentives and penalties between reforms in education and reforms in other sectors.

Unlike macroeconomic adjustment, quality education reforms do not engender immediate tangible political gains to governments. Many benefits of improved education are often imperceptible in the immediate term. In contrast, changes in the macroeconomy are visible within months, allowing politicians to capitalize on these accomplishments in the near term. As Geddes argues, incumbent politicians are interested in maximizing their career goals, which normally means enhancing their chance, or that of their allies, of winning upcoming elections.

In New Zealand, the Prime Minister took over the Ministry and appointed a reform specialist to lead the effort. In El Salvador, by inviting presidential candidates to participate in various fora to discuss the reforms, reform advocates succeeded in getting presidential candidates to consider education reform as a primary issue in the 1994 elections -immediate electoral concerns of politicians and the long-term results of education reform gives rise to shortcomings in governmental commitment.

Moreover, many governments traditionally relied on educational systems as mechanisms for political co-optation. Teaching positions are treated as a form of employment of last resort, very often in compensation for some type of political favor. Mexico is a good example. Following the 1968 massacre of students, the Mexican government attempted to alleviate student discontent by launching a massive expansion of the education sector.

The Mexican government has also used the education sector to cushion the impact of economic adversity. Teachers' unions, on the other hand, are often led by professional politicians who tend to make their careers in union activism. Thus, unlike most ministers of education, leaders of teachers' unions have longer time horizons and no alternative or next-step career objectives. Moreover, leaders of teachers' union tend to come from leftist parties, which place a premium on challenging the state.

The magnetism and high levels of organization of teachers' unions, together with a union leadership that has a long-term horizon, no alternative career plan, no aversion to conflict, and a discriminating weapon against the government, explain why teachers' unions are to be expected to be intensely active in resisting reforms.

In order to explain the greater extent of decentralization in health than in education in Venezuela, González uses a similar analysis of the different cost-impact and bargaining power of affected interest groups. Many quality reforms entail some form of decentralization, which raises a whole new set of political difficulties. Decentralization involves the transfer of decision-making authority for planning management, and transferring resources from the central government to outer tiers of governments or units such as provinces, municipalities, local councils, or autonomous entities . The problem is that, although many governments have embarked on decentralization projects since the late 1970s, they can never be counted on to be fully committed to the presumed objectives of decentralization.

As Weiler shows, the three main arguments for advancing decentralizationCredistributing power, enhancing efficience of public services, and improving learningCconflict directly with the inherent interest of states to retain and centralize authority. This clash between the inherent interest of states and the inherent goals of decentralization complicates the politics of reform implementation through at least three mechanisms. First, government commitment to decentralization is likely to be insincere or at least motivated by the wrong reasons.

Decentralization challenges the power and authority of these bureaucrats. In addition, bureaucrats are a source of inertia because the organization of power in bureaucracies does not place a premium on individual initiative. Bureaucrats are expected to follow orders and procedures, but they are seldom rewarded for learning, initiating, and solving problems, which are critical aspects of any reform initiative. For these reasons, the most virulent and successful reform enemies are not always the teachers' unions, but professional bureaucrats.

The main problem with an analysis of the reforms based on solely cost-benefit impact, on the powers and incidence of policy entrepreneurs, and the mixed motives of central authorities is that it overstates its caseCit overpredicts reform paralysis. However, the empirical evidence in the last 20 years contradicts this pessimistic prediction. Numerous cases of quality reforms have been approved and implemented throughout the world. These cases were selected for illustration purposes. Although they were not randomly selected, these cases represent various regions of the world and various levels of educational and economic development.

Any political strategies or institutional setting that adresses any of these problems should, in principle, enhance the likelihood of reform implementation. The hypotheses are grouped into three broad categories: 1) hypotheses about type and style of reform; 2) hypotheses about political strategies to either bolster the supply or the demand for reform; and 3) hypotheses about institutional features that magnify or diminish the power of reform opponents.

In Poland, the economic reforms produced a short-term rise in unemployment, which may have compelled government officials to slow down education reform (government officials might have concluded that this was not the best time to produce reforms that entail lay offs). Moreover, the education sector has always been seen as an "employer of last resort," all the more reason to stop reforms at the time. In Chile, a new democratic government in the 1990s refused to deepen many of the quality and systemic reforms introduced by the dictatorship in the 1980s (e.g., voucher system).

In some areas, it has actually undone some reforms (e.g., municipalities have lost the right to fire teachers). One reason for these setbacks is that the government felt that teachers, who would have borne the brunt of reform deepening and who constituted significant electoral support of the new government, suffered enough during the previous reforms, and thus, deserved some compensation.

In Romania education reforms have made more progress than in Poland. This too might have something to do with Romania's lower turnover rate at the ministry of education. There is thus evidence to believe that a strong supply of reform initiative, stemming from low ministerial turnover rates, can counteract even unstable, polarized, and complex political situation.

South-east Asian countries constitute the classic example of the presumed connection between openness to the global economy and the implementation of quality reform education. In the 1960s, several Southeast Asian countries began to adopt export-oriented economic model of development. Governments throughout the region realized that in order to gain an exporting edge in highly competitive world markets, they needed to raise the educational level of their work force.

In Romania, a National Council for the Reform of Education was created, comprised of leading intellectuals interested in educational questions. In New Zealand, a commission (the Picot Commission) was established in 1987 to suggest reforms, with the unusual feature that its leader was not an education specialist, but a businessman.

In El Salvador, an advisory council including 50 representatives from 30 different groups was created during the assessment stages. Stakeholders were required to submit position papers to these councils. The councils proved so successful in keeping the pace of reforms that the minister, initially skeptical, decided to extend the life of the council during the implementation stages.

In South Korea in February 1994, a Committee on the Education Reform Implementation was set up to monitor the implementation of reforms launched that year. Certain commonalities emerge from these cases. It seems that to be effective, these independent advisory/evaluative bodies must be composed of representatives from civil society, not just politicians. In addition, membership in these consultative councils should not be subject to high turnover. Including respected intellectual leaders bolsters the credibility and respectability of the council, opinion-makers such as journalists link the reform process to media outlets, and think-tank experts signal technocratic competence. In some cases (e.g., Uruguay), including technocrats from international organizations (CEPAL) helped politically because it signaled impartiality and competence.

In Thailand, community leaders helped disseminate information concerning the school, and made suggestions regarding how the schools might contribute to the community. Independent advisory councils are not panaceas, but they can perform crucial political tasks. First, the respectability of its members infuses the reform effort with credibility, thus contributing to societal acceptance of the reforms. Second, the presence of journalists and intellectuals establishes links between the reformers and the opinion-making sector, thus increasing the chance that local commentators become both stakeholders as well as frequent writers on the topic. Third, and most important, it counteracts the expected shortcomings in the supply of reform initiative.

In some cases, for instance, heads of state instruct their ministers of education to follow the directives of these independent councils. Setting up a formally constituted group with longer time horizons, nonevident alternative career plans and interest in the reform can act as an effective counterbalance to the negative side-effect of high ministerial turnover.

In South Korea, for instance, despite the bolstering of the supply of reform, teachers remain fairly unsupportive of the reform effort. Mechanisms for gaining societal allies and neutralizing the reform opponents are still necessary. Despite the stronger demand for quality education reform, the political force of this demand is likely to remain relatively weak. Effective implementation requires counteracting this weakness on the demand side.

In New Zealand, for instance, the government established working parties, which met regularly at the local level to seek consensus on reform implementation. A similar tactic was used in El Salvador in 1993, at a time when societal enthusiasm for the reforms was waning. Local reformers, together with a team from the Harvard Institute for International Development (HIID), began to hold a series of meetings and workshops with local actors, civic leaders, business leaders, journalists, ministerial staff, etc. One of these meetings involved the presidential candidates.

As a result, the opposition party endorsed the-reform, and since then, the reforms became a key electoral issue in the elections. This was a well-timed strategy of dissemination and inclusion that counteracted a slack in societal enthusiasm. In Uruguay, another case of relative implementation success, the office in charge of the reforms also conducted a massive information campaign once the program of reform was designed. These efforts succeeded in convincing the citizenry about the need for deep reforms, not a trivial accomplishment considering that in the late 1980s few citizens treated education reform as an urgent matter.

In Pakistan, one of the reasons for the success of the Mosque-program was the explicit incorporation of religious sector, the Imams, who were given a direct role in the schools. In Thailand, the government carried out an all-out effort to include Alocal providers and consumers of education in the implementation process. Teachers and school administrators were brought in to help design a diversified curriculum; administrators, parents and students were called on to assess its success.

In 1989, Colombia's Congress approved legislation giving municipalities a greater role in basic services, culminating in the 1991 Constitution, which called for one of the most far-reaching decentralization mandates in Latin America, including deep education decentralization. Although some reforms were implemented between 1991 and 1994, the key components of the reformsCapproval of school autonomy and the municipalization of basic educationCwere blocked in part due to resistance from the leading teachers union (FECODE), a highly organized and centralized union with more than 200,000 members.

Although government officials went out of their way to negotiate, they failed to persuade FECODE. If anything, the inclusion of FECODE in policy deliberation sent the wrong signals to Congressional leaders. It led them to overestimate the level of societal opposition to reform. As a result, both Congress and the Minister of Education changed their minds about the desirability of deep education reforms. New legislation was adopted in 1993 and 1994 that watered down the decentralization process.

In Poland in 1993, the 300,000-strong Polish Teachers' Union (ZNP) strongly resisted the government's effort to reform the education sector, which called for decentralizing secondary education and introducing a performance-related promotion system for teachers. To placate this opposition, the government appointed a ZNP leader as deputy prime minister of education in 1994 and promised to raise teacher salaries. All to no avail. ZNP opposition remained as unyielding as ever, eventually forcing the minister of education (Kazimierz Marcinkiewicz) to resign.

In short, teachers' unions play a crucial role in education reform. Teachers' unions often perceive these reforms as involving serious material and political sacrifices on their part. This might make them hostile to the reforms. Compared to other cost-bearers, teachers' unions enjoy comparative political advantages—Corganization, centralization, and coverage of a broad constituency. Thus, if they turn against the reforms, teachers' unions can seriously undermine the process.

For these reasons, reform implementation is contingent on the cooperation of teacher's unions, or at least, in preventing them from derailing the reform process. Under certain conditions, the hands of governments are tied. Whether unions cooperate or not might depend on institutional factors that are beyond the control of reformers. Under other conditions, however, governments can significantly affect the propensity of unions to cooperate.

Political scientists frequently stress that the characteristics of a country's political institutions play a crucial role in the implementation of reforms. Countries 'that have fragmented and polarized political parties, for instance, face greater governability problems. Even when parties are strong, the party system could be highly polarized, which also hampers implementation. Under such conditions, unions with strong historical and institutional links to opposition parties are likely to turn more hostile, in part because government-union relations will merely reflect the polarized nature of government-union relations.

2

Curriculum Change as a Reform Strategy

In a more practical and technological sense, a retroactive orientation to the improvement of educational systems, depends on monitoring and evaluation provisions. In retroactive planning the improvement process is driven by evaluation-feedback mechanisms. A wide range of approaches to educational monitoring & evaluation (M&E) is available. These approaches are determined by:

— the key function of M&E;

— the kind of data source;

— the level of application.

Educational M&E can be carried out in function of:

— certification and accreditation;

— accountability, either in the form of 'consumerism' or administrative control;

— organisational learning.

Educational systems are hierarchical systems, with levels ranging from the national government to the individual student. In order to visualise how systemic M&E could be the motor of enhanced performance of educational systems, some assumptions concerning the patterns of centralisation and decentralisation should be made, first of all. The concept of functional decentralisation expresses that systems may be centralised in one domain, for example the domain of educational standards, and decentralised in another, such as the domain of instruction.

A realistic option for primary and (lower) secondary education is a standardisation of educational outcomes by centrally stating educational objectives and achievement standards. At the same time in all other domains considerable decentralisation could take place. In such a situation outcome attainment at the level of the system, schools and individual students could be monitored on the basis of examination and educational testing systems. Modern techniques for item-banking could create considerable synergy in the construction and use of assessment instruments.

The way the information could be used and fed back to various actors should be carefully considered, applications would range from harsh 'control' measures, to milder incentives and sanctions and 'coaching'. Other types of monitoring and evaluation could be based on review and inquiry methods directed at an analysis of means and conditions. These could be done either externally, for example by inspectorates, or internally, by school staff. Ideally learning processes at the basic levels of the education system should be evoked, by reflecting on the results of certain mixes of M&E methods.

In this way M&E instruments could provide practical handles to make a vague ideal in the sense of 'schools as learning organisations' more realistic. At higher education levels, vocational secondary schools and tertiary education, scanning mechanisms for adapting goals to societal requirements could be situated at lower levels of the system, for example at the level of regional centres. Focussing on M&E and feedback mechanisms as a lever for improvement of the functioning of educational systems, does not mean that other kinds of inputs should be overlooked.

Particularly in developing countries basic material and human resource conditions are a primary concern. Curriculum development and teacher training are likewise areas that are very important. Ideally all components should be well integrated, of course. The suggestion that is made here is that assessment, monitoring and evaluation tools could be taken on first, instead of last, in the planning of educational reform.

In developing countries, there are all kinds of limiting pre-conditions. Limitations in the technical infrastructure and human capacity is the first category of pre-conditions that comes to mind. But, in addition, organisational and institutional capabilities should be taken into consideration. To the extent that human capacity is available it is often locked up in fragmented organisational structures, where coordination is totally lacking. Institutional capacity in the domain of educational M&E refers to the presence or absence of legislation concerning quality control, but also to a more elusive notion of the presence of an 'evaluation culture'. Last but not least the real application of M&E in education may suffer from political constraints and political bias in the conduct of use of M&E methods.

At the level of national educational systems, development of M&E provisions is not likely to run ahead of provisions in domains like teacher training and curriculum development; although an integrated approach to these major levers of systemic improvement (training, curriculum development and assessment/ evaluation) seems attractive.

Students' everyday experiences in school were seen as operating to socialize students to accept their future positions in the larger social order. Thus, the hidden curriculum of schools played an important role in class reproduction. A newer tradition in sociological studies of curriculum has uncovered clear connections between exposure to curriculum and student learning. Barr and Dreeben viewed the school as a system of nested layers, in which outputs at one level of school organization serve as inputs for the next. In this view curriculum is an element of the technology of instruction, allocated from administrators to teachers, who exert some degree of autonomy in providing access to curriculum to students.

Barr and Dreeben showed that curriculum coverage in first-grade reading instruction exerts substantial effects on students' learning to read. The more new words teachers introduced, the more words students learned to read, and the better they could read at the end of the year. Similarly, Rowan and Miracle found that teachers who covered more stories in the reading curriculum produced more learning among their elementary school students. Gamoran also showed that coverage of the reading curriculum largely accounted for the effects of ability grouping in first-grade reading.

Evidence for the importance of curriculum is equally strong at the secondary level. A variety of studies show that students who take more academic courses, and especially, more advanced academic courses, gain more on achievement tests. These effects seem especially strong in mathematics and science, where achievement differences among students in different tracks is largely a consequence of differential course-taking.

Bryk, Lee, and Holland attributed the achievement advantages of Catholic over public high schools to the more focused and rigorous academic curriculum of Catholic high schools. Consistent with this claim, Gamoran observed less inequality between tracks in Catholic compared with public high schools, presumably because Catholic high schools provide a demanding academic curriculum even to students outside the academic track. In light of these findings, it is important to ask whether manipulating the curriculum could serve as a potent policy lever for raising student achievement.

If particular emphasis is placed on increasing the richness and rigor of the curriculum available to low-achieving students, will that reduce the learning deficit suffered by such students over time? It may seem obvious that students cannot learn what they have not been taught, but this key point has failed to receive much attention in many plans for restructuring and reform. In contrast to many other countries, the curriculum in the United States is relatively undifferentiated. Almost all students study in comprehensive high schools, and there are relatively few formal divisions within schools.

Nonetheless, differentiation occurs in American schools, ranging from reading groups in the early elementary years to varied course assignments in secondary schools. Although contemporary high schools rarely have formally identified tracking structures, the vast majority of schools divide students on some measure of ability for at least some subjects. When high schools sort students into honors, regular, and basic classes, curriculum and instruction are differentiated, and student achievement becomes correspondingly more unequal over time.

The aim of transition courses is to bring low-achieving students into the college-preparatory pipeline. Because curriculum differentiation leads to achievement inequality, one may suppose that standardizing the curriculum would provide greater support for equity. There are few if any models of large-scale curriculum standardization in the United States, and certainly none with a closely related examination system. To assess the impact of curriculum standardization, we need to look outside the United States.

In Scotland during the 1980s, an important reform of the secondary curriculum, called "Standard Grade," took place. Whereas students had previously been divided into academic and nonacademic courses of study, the Standard Grade reform brought all students into academic courses. In response to the problems of lower-level mathematics classes described above, many states and districts are working to improve the quality of the mathematics curriculum for low-achieving students.

The most recent and dramatic example of this effort is New York City's decision to require all students to enroll in academic math and science courses in the first two years of high school. The New York City initiative is just getting under way, and assessment of the program is not yet possible, though early indications suggest that the program is being implemented. In Buffalo, courses from the University of Chicago School Mathematics Project

(UCSMP) served as an alternative to the Regents math sequence. UCSMP was adopted to counter the high failure rates in Regents courses. The first course in the UCSMP sequence, called "Transition Math," is analogous to the other courses we studied, in that it provides a bridge between elementary and college-preparatory mathematics.

UCSMP stresses an integrated mathematics content, including applied arithmetic, algebra, geometry, logic, probability, and statistics. Like Math A, the course emphasizes problem solving and real-world applications. A sign of success for UCSMP Transition Math would be high proportions of students pursuing a college-preparatory curriculum.

Until the early 1980s, Scottish secondary students were selected for academic study in the Ordinary Grade (O Grade) courses. Students who were not selected for O Grade courses could not take the corresponding examinations, and thus had no chance for further academic study in secondary school, let alone higher education. In an effort to broaden access to academic study, the Scottish education system implemented the Standard Grade reform beginning in the mid-1980s. Unlike the O Grade system, in which students were selectively enrolled in academic courses, the Standard Grade reform encouraged all students to take academic courses and to sit for the corresponding national examinations about age sixteen.

Standard Grade courses were not totally undifferentiated-some grouping occurred into levels called foundation, general, and credit-but these levels were mixed in most schools, most students sat for two levels of the examinations (i.e., foundation and general, or general and credit), and the system was far less differentiated than the academic versus nonacademic divide that had characterized the O Grade system.

On average, controlling for gender, social background, and school context, examination scores rose in English, mathematics, and the sciences during the period of the implementation of Standard Grade in these subjects. This rise was due in part to the reform itself: Scores rose faster in schools that implemented Standard Grade first. Moreover, the unequal distribution of examination results diminished over the same period. Within years, social inequality of achievement within schools was less in schools that implemented Standard Grade, compared with schools that had not.

Inequality within schools declined because disadvantaged students had better opportunities to enroll in academic courses, and they usually obtained awards in the subjects they studied. At one level, the Standard Grade reform has been dramatically successful. More students than ever are studying academic curricula and are obtaining awards on the national examinations. There is also less inequality within schools in who participates in academic study. These changes are, in part, a direct result of the reform.

If we think about the education system as a ladder, then the Standard Grade reform allowed many more students to step onto the ladder. It has not, however, taken them all to the top of the ladder. Inequality remains at the highest levels of schooling. There are some signs that inequality in access to postsecondary education may be diminishing.

Paterson, using data through 1994, observed a decline in social inequality of students going directly from secondary to higher education. This trend may be an indirect result of the Standard Grade reform, if the broader accumulation of academic qualifications has created greater demand for access to higher education, but it is difficult to confirm this speculation empirically. Whether or not Standard Grade has played a role in postsecondary expansion, it has clearly opened up the possibility of high levels of educational attainment for students who would formerly have been excluded.

Irrespective of its role in postsecondary education, the impact of Standard Grade at the secondary level, both for examinations and for staying on, is significant for several reasons. First, academic study has value in its own right, stimulating students' intellectual development. Second, receiving awards on national examinations, even if they are not at the top levels, helps students in a wide range of subsequent activities, including employment and training. Third, Standard Grade removed the stigma of nonacademic study from the last years of compulsory schooling, as reforms currently underway in Scotland are attempting to accomplish for postcompulsory secondary schooling.

Clearly, curriculum has an impact on student learning. Moreover, curriculum can be manipulated. Consequently, changes in curriculum-across classes, across schools, and over time-lead to changes in student achievement. These findings are consistent with Barr and Dreeben's organizational conception of schools, in which curriculum is a technological tool wielded by teachers to stimulate student learning. Policymakers seeking leverage over learning would do well to consider curriculum change as a path to improvement.

Indeed, curriculum change has been under consideration for some time in U.S. policy circles. Standards for curriculum and assessment are widely discussed at the national, state, and local levels across the country. Beyond increased high school course-work requirements, little actual headway has been made in reforming curricula on a large scale. A major problem for curriculum reform in this country is the absence of widely recognized examinations that are tied to the curriculum. In countries with articulated systems of curriculum and examinations, such as Scotland, the curriculum is a serious entity, not to be trifled with or ignored.

In the United States, only normative pressures sustain some degree of curricular coherence from one locale to the next. Curriculum reforms without assessments are likely to be weakly implemented and thus to have modest effects. As Smith and O'Day argued, systemic reform calls for an alignment of curriculum and assessment. Statewide assessments, for example, would make state curricular reforms much more powerful than commonly occurs at present. In this sense, the context of curriculum reform is likely to make a substantial difference for the effects of curriculum reform.

Role of Universities

Universities in developing countries are to be powerful instruments for national development is now generally accepted. At the same time there is also a predominant disenchantment with the way universities do actually contribute to development. One of the causes for that limited contribution is the institutional weakness of many universities. In Africa, University leaders, donors and

Northern partners should shift some attention and funding from academic development to institutional strengthening in the sense of improved policy development, governance, management and planning. This will also improve the effectiveness, quality and, particularly, the sustainability of individual academic cooperation projects.

Another important aspect in cooperation between donor agencies, Northern universities and universities in developing countries which will have to be taken into account more than has been the case so far, generally, is the issue of enhancing ownership in the formulation of cooperation programs. Enhanced ownership is expected to render results and make effects of cooperation more sustainable. Northern and Southern partners together should develop mechanisms that will actually strengthen ownership and recognise the available strengths within Southern institutions.

The role of the universities in the South is in its various components not different from that of universities in Northern countries. It can be phrased in several ways, varying from simply teaching, research and community service to crucial instruments for democratisation and the creation of a civil society.

Higher education institutes have the main responsibility for equipping individuals with the advanced knowledge and skills required for the highest positions in government, business and the professions. Universities are the main channels for the transfer, adaptation and dissemination of knowledge. In this way they provide both public services and private enterprise with the information and knowledge they need.

Universities foster a sense of national identity and are often in the forefront of democratic and other social developments. Investments in higher education can be a key contributor to a country's economic growth. All these components of the role of the universities contribute to national development, but for the universities in the South this was not considered to be enough. The universities in the South had, were perceived to have, or thought that they ought to have a unique role in shaping the new nations they were part of. Their missions should be directly relevant to national needs.

The notion of the university with an explicit focus on development has now left the level of politicians and has firmly taken root with university leaders. The University has drawn up its own strategic development plan with broad consultation of the whole university community and outside stakeholders. The computerisation of the libraries and the historical archives is at an advanced stage. With the frustration, exasperation, irritation and concern about the decline of African higher education these sorts of accomplishments, and the circumstances and the time in which they have been made, should not be forgotten.

Nonetheless Africa's universities currently stand in crisis at a crucial point in their development. There are serious concerns about the future form and substance of higher education in Africa. There is general disenchantment with the progress made with regard to the Development University. This can of course be explained: against the factors favouring a developmental emphasis in universities, there are several weighty limitations. Factors that could favour a developmental emphasis in the universities included:

1. Sense of national and civic responsibility of universities and their staff;
2. Government incentives and policies;
3. University self-interest in the context of government and donor policies;
4. Donor community policies over the last three decades, despite the critical re-appraisal of university aid policies in the 70's.

The universities did try with varying degrees of conviction, imagination and drive to enhance the social relevance of what they were doing:

— they tried to expand their role in extension work and community service;

— they tried to contribute more to national policy development;

— they tried to adapt to the manpower needs of the society, particularly the need for more graduates in the sciences and technological subjects;

— and they tried to play a part in national integration, by ameliorating ethnic, class or regional inequalities.

The greatest limitation to the universities of the South in fulfilling their role as Development Universities is found, however, in a severely hampered institutional development, going hand in hand with the general decline of African higher education. And societal relevance, to fulfil the expectations of the Development University is very difficult when the university does not have its own house in order.

The limited success of African institutes for higher education at developing an outreach role was largely because they were fully preoccupied first with the issues of institutional development and later with the far more encompassing general crisis in African tertiary education.

In most developing countries higher education exhibits severe deficiencies, in many, particularly in Sub Saharan Africa, tertiary education is in actual decline. The decline shows itself in such issues as educational quality;

— relevance of curricula; inadequate job performance;

— an output mix with a dominance in the social sciences and arts, which contributes to graduate unemployment;

— inefficient use of resources;

— high repetition and drop out rates; the quality, quantity and relevance of research output; and

— student unrest and staff frustration, causing internal or external brain drain.

While the scale and shape of the deficiencies or decline vary from country to country, university to university and even from faculty to faculty, several common factors account for the general erosion of many universities:

— The original set-up was lavish, produced very high unit costs and was too expensive to maintain.

— The demographic explosion and increased public demand for higher education.

— The failure of many national economies, which puts a ceiling on educational budgets, that need to be shared with the expanding primary and secondary school systems.

— Minimal national investment in research.

— Deteriorating primary and secondary schooling.

— A sometimes adverse political context.

— Insufficient managerial systems.

— The complexities of a great variety of donor policies.

And so the enormous problems facing higher education hamper institutional development of the universities, which in turn makes it difficult for them to play the expected part in national development.

Support to universities in the South and particularly in Sub Saharan Africa has been aimed not directly at realising the notion of the Development University, but at institutional development more generally, and that mostly through particular forms of cooperation: scholarships for studies in the North and academic cooperation projects. The Dutch government and the Netherlands Organisation for International Cooperation in Higher Education (Nuffic) were guided, just as other assistance agencies such as the Rockefeller Foundation, by the concept of institution building which we perceived to have its own justification.

Support that enabled universities to do more effective teaching, reflection and research and to produce specialised manpower was by definition a contribution to development. Implicitly we were aiming for national development, in particular poverty alleviation, institutional development, and the academic development of chosen departments and chosen persons. All at the same time, with any clear favourites. One of the most tried and respected means of institution building is the inter-institutional linkage: linkages between institutes for higher education in the North and in the South.

In most linkage programs, including our Dutch programs institution building has mainly been targeted at academic developments: improvement of curricula, joint research projects, scholarships for staff upgrading, teaching and training by foreigners and the supply of material goods to refurbish a laboratory, stock a library or to provide transport. And as such almost always on department or faculty level. For many years the long-term aim was to have these linkages grow into academic cooperation schemes between equal partners.

Many universities both in the North and in the South are more interested in joint academic projects than in efforts to improve governance and management. In the North this is because most academics are not involved in management and the managers are not involved in collaboration with tertiary institutions in developing countries. Universities in the South are interesting for scientific cooperation, but until recently rarely as laboratories for management studies. In the South administrators and executives are not too keen to be the object of a development project to improve governance and management.

Nonetheless, all parties were convinced that something had to be done to improve the situation in the Southern universities, if only to meet the most immediate challenge, that of finding ways of meeting the high and increasing costs of educating ever growing numbers of students, while at the same time maintaining and improving the quality of education and research. In setting up the Institutional Development Programme of the Dutch government, the Nuffic elaborated, in close consultation with all stakeholders, the following concepts for the Joint Financing Programme for Cooperation in Higher Education (MHO):

1. National governments and university leaders recognise that the first and foremost condition to reach the institutional strength needed to be able to take on the multifarious challenges is increased attention to governance, management and administration. Universities must open up to national governments and enter into dialogues with them and their other stakeholders.

2. Assistance agencies need to join efforts. Donor co-ordination, which at the level of an African university must be dealt with by the university management, must assume new dimensions in the sense that donors should set a common agenda for institutional reform.

3. The way in which we have thought to come to grips with all that is through the now generally accepted concept of ownership. And ownership on central level.

The financial crisis in most African countries during the past decades has made it difficult for governments to meet their obligations in the higher education sector. Donor agencies have contributed to efforts to sustain African higher education during the past two/three decades. North-South cooperation has been an important component of donor supported cooperation. In order for the North - South cooperation to be more effective and sustainable, it is important to find effective strategies and appropriate methods for building sustainable innovation capacity in Higher Education institutions in the South.

The global education market will have effects on access to education, grip on content, cultural identity and relevance of teaching and research to local circumstances of many countries. Together with the growth of

Information and Communication Technologies this will make it improbable that academic cooperation for development will continue to maintain the shape and form it has had over the last decades.

3

Community Role in School Reforms

Schools' efforts to respond, whether they choose to do so or whether they are required to do so, are commendable. Most educators and most families care deeply about the children in their charge. But whereas families are able to focus all their love and attention on their own children, every day educators face the challenge of focusing on individual children who come to school from each of many different families. This is reality. This is life. The expectations of families are essential for good parenting, and the challenges to educators are part and parcel of the vocation they chose.

Communities also have great expectations of schools, but communities include many families who either do not have school-age children or who choose to educate their children in ways other than sending them to public schools. In most communities these families are in the majority. What they know about the public schools comes primarily from three sources:

(1) relatives, friends, neighbors, acquaintances, and workplace colleagues;

(2) the local news media; and

(3) teachers and administrators who work for the local school system.

Relatively few members of the wider community have direct, current experience with the public schools. For others, their understanding of the schools is an amalgam of correct information, misinformation, impressions, nostalgia, skepticism, and wishful thinking. This is reality. This is life. Most communities believe public education should be better than they perceive it to be, though most families think the schools their children attend are good or better. Both are right.

Public schools do a much better job than most people give them credit for, but public schools and the students they serve should be performing at much higher levels. It would be wonderful if more public schools acknowledged this, and aggressively pursued reform. Unfortunately, they have been slow to do so. Communities have not done much better. Most communities believe school reform is necessary, even if they are not quite sure what it means or what it will require.

Many communities support reform so long as educators and other people's children bear the brunt of it. Some communities respond positively to civic leaders who make school reform their mission, but few communities have made the effort to join with educators to develop and subsequently support a substantive reform agenda. Among those that have, fewer still have had the patience to remain focused on reform through all the advances and setbacks that are part of any meaningful change process.

However, school reform that results in significantly higher levels of performance by both educators and students will not occur if it is only a few elected officials and education and business leaders demand it, understand it, support it, and monitor it.

Without broad-based support by the community as a whole, school reform will either be short lived or have limited effect. What, then, is necessary for communities to become more active partners in the reform process? First, they need partners in the person of education leaders, notably school board members, superintendents, and principals, who candidly identify the weaknesses of their school systems and schools. Not all education leaders recognize these shortcomings and many would do well to be more attentive to what their communities' often try to tell them.

Communities are not always right, but their day-to-day encounters with their school systems and schools can be very instructive. For communities to be engaged in reform, they first have to experience that education leaders are making the effort to listen to and learn from them. At the same time, communities have to act as though they believe education leaders will respond and act in good faith, even if their previous experience gives them little reason for such hope.

Developing this level of trust is not easy for either party, but there can be no partnership until there is deep, sustained communication. This takes a lot of work, and many times it cannot occur unless a neutral party facilitates it. Organizations such as the Collaborative Communications Group, The Harwood Institute, KSA Plus Communications, or Public Agenda can provide this type of assistance. While such organizations can help launch and facilitate a process of civil discourse, it is a community's responsibility to build on these experiences by creating and sustaining venues in which communities and educators will not only share information about difficult education issues, but also develop and execute plans for resolving them.

If the challenges of such reporting are too daunting for local news media, then other groups must fill this vacuum. Some community organizations seek to play this role by conducting independent research and publishing special in-depth reports on important education issues. There are situations in which a community's efforts to improve its communications with school officials and learn more about the challenges facing educators and children do not result in the actions necessary to improve schools.

Communities can do many things to be constructive partners in the change process, but when all is said and done educators are the stewards for the public schools. In the best cases, but within many limitations imposed on them, educators respond to their community's concerns. When this is not the case, communities have little recourse except to take action. They can, for example, become political and seek to change the voting majority on the school board. Individual citizens need to have the generosity of spirit to look beyond their own pocketbooks and whether they currently have children in school. No community will prosper if its civic action is immobilized by the narrow self-interests of citizens whose commitment to education ends at their front doors.

No school system will reform if its communities do not clearly, forcefully, and consistently communicate their specific expectations for what they want public education to help their children achieve. No children will perform at levels higher than they believe possible if communities and schools do not work together to provide every child, in every class, in every school, a challenging curricula and quality teachers every day. Improving the results schools achieve is not a task for the timid, whether the actors are educators or communities. Schools will not improve unless the knowledge, skills, and practice of educators improve.

Schools will improve only marginally unless the knowledge, skills, and practice of communities also improve. This means learning more about schools, identifying and recognizing their good practices, and identifying and demanding the correction of their ineffective practices. For ordinary citizens this is a major challenge because about the most many of them can do is raise and guide their children, and pay the taxes that enable public schools to function. Yet, these citizens do see, they do hear, they do talk, they do feel, they do understand.

It is the responsibility of communities to provide reliable information so citizens will learn what their schools are doing and how well they are doing it, to provide venues where the voices of these citizens will be heard, to support their efforts to organize and act if school officials do not respond, and to partner with educators so they will make the changes necessary to educate all children well.

International Education Cooperation

Developing high-quality education for all to benefit remains a formidable task in many parts of the world. Opening school doors to all children, including marginalised groups such as ethnic minorities, and providing quality education that allows them to develop lifelong learning skills is still something to be achieved in the future. This is especially the case in countries where financial resources are limited, and where malnutrition, child labour, HIV/AIDS and civil wars have a severe impact on children's chances to participate in education.

Keeping children in school and providing them with relevant educational experiences, recruiting sufficient teachers and improving the quality of the teaching force, developing a good and reliable monitoring system, and strengthening institutional management and accountability, are just a few of the many challenges these countries are faced with.

Multi-faceted reform strategies are needed to address the challenges in expanding access and improving quality. Policy strategies require a clear vision on education improvement as well as realistic timelines and investments. Comprehensive reform programs are needed that address the improvement of basic conditions for learning, of curricula and assessment procedures, and of teacher development in a coherent and consistent way. This calls for more collaboration between stakeholders in the field and a strengthening of linkages between the macro-, meso- and micro-levels in the education system.

The development of systemic reform programs requires strong central leadership. Within ministries in many developing countries there is often limited room to manoeuvre due to financial constraints and the lack of management and implementation capacity. Moreover, donor involvement is often hard to orchestrate, leading to fragmentation in policy development and implementation. To enhance local ownership of development programs and to provide a better context for a more systemic planning of education, many countries now have adopted sector-wide approaches to education reform.

In this approach a broad policy framework is developed in which governments and donor organisations work in partnership, with local governments taking the lead in policy formation and planning. A sector-wide approach (ideally) involves extensive consultation of stakeholders in the design of coherent policy programs at various levels in the education system. While this approach provides good opportunities to enhance synergy between stakeholders, it also creates new learning needs as well as new demands for national planning and implementation capacity at all levels in the system. Issues to be considered include how to achieve wide local ownership, and how best to support the capacity to design and manage sector-wide approaches.

The current challenge for international education cooperation will be to attend to these issues and take the opportunity of working towards systemic and sustainable reform with enhanced local ownership and capacity. The body of knowledge on international education development, especially regarding successful interventions and processes, still needs further elaboration and articulation. While there is a great deal to be learned from the wealth of international experiences, policy strategies are often not built on insights from other contexts and the wheel is reinvented many times. Enhancing the capacity to learn from experiences and building more effective international learning communities is therefore of crucial importance.

Sharing knowledge and expertise regarding capacity building is the main mission of the Dutch Expertise Consortium for International Development of Education

(DECIDE). This consortium was established in 1999 by the Vrije Universiteit Amsterdam (International Cooperation Centre) and the University of Twente (Faculty of Behavioural Sciences and CHEPS) with the aim of joining forces in international educational development. DECIDE's three main areas of activity include education and training, consultancy and development, and research and evaluation.

The major characteristics of education and training are degree programs in Educational Training and Systems design, Human Resources Development and Telematics applications. In addition, tailor-made courses are organised on issues related to curriculum, professional development and institutional management for policymakers, teacher educators and other professionals from a variety of countries. Research and evaluation activities focus on curriculum and staff development, management development and quality assurance in education, and ICT and educational development.

Activities mainly include doctoral projects, shorter studies, research partnerships, and research networking. In consultancy and development, DECIDE has a primary focus on curriculum development and educational change, teacher training and staff development, monitoring, assessment and quality assurance, ICT, and improvement of science education. Activities include both short-term consultancies as well as long-term collaboration projects with universities in Tanzania, Mozambique and Bolivia. These projects include staff development, curriculum development and implementation, research at MSc and PhD level and institutional strengthening.

Since its initiation in 1999, there has been a rapid expansion of activities in all three domains. The number of consortium partners has grown through participation by other Dutch universities, research institutes and expertise institutes in the field of education development. In international activities and in deliberations with consortium partners in the past years, several questions have arisen regarding international education cooperation.

In fact, based on the record of the last century alone, one could argue convincingly that learning in broad-based education systems must lie at the heart of any national transformation that succeeds and endures. In our contemporary global setting, it is scarcely any wonder then that education is high on the political agenda of each and every country. Many election campaigns in recent years have been won or lost over the issue of education. An instructive example comes from the recent British General Election of 2001, vividly illustrated by a cartoon in the Financial Times of August 31, 2001.

It depicts Prime Minister, Tony Blair who focused on education and health as main issues for his re-election campaign in the U.K. It is a poignant illustration of the political centrality of education and yet one could point to many other high-income countries where education played a major role in election campaigns.

But, equally, in developing countries, education is an issue with a tremendous political constituency. In Uganda, for example, President Museveni successfully used education in the election campaign of 2001, to amplify his claims of substantial progress in key sectors. This recent revival of the key role of education in the minds of voters should not come as a surprise. When people are asked about their priorities in life, they rank the education of their children and their personal health highly, together with personal and financial security.

So the real surprise is why it took so long for both developing and developed nations to express the urgency for giving access to all children to quality education in Jomtien in 1990. Even more surprising was the lack of progress in implementing the Jomtien Declaration, which aimed at helping all children of the relevant age group to have access to primary education of good quality. The global community has committed itself firmly to the notion that every child and every adult should get the chance to learn to read and write and to achieve basic numeracy. It is widely accepted that these skills are an essential prerequisite both for democracy and for development.

The primacy of education in development was re-affirmed by the September 2000 UN Millennial Summit, which generated a set of Millennium Development Goals, two of which relate directly to education's role in reducing poverty and empowering people:

— Every child should participate in primary education by 2015;

— Gender disparities in education should be eliminated by 2005.

Education for All

There is no doubt that whatever one's talents are, a youngster's education has a tremendous positive impact on his or her cultural, social and material prosperity in later life. Quality education is truly the gateway to participation in society, as.well as to better paid jobs, as outlined in the World Bank's Education Sector Strategy. Education as an investment in human capital yields a return in the labour market. Nevertheless, virtually all studies find that wages increase significantly with educational attainment. There are potentially significant returns to education among non-wage workers as well.

Some studies focus on the potential credentialing effect of education - whereby schooling signals ability rather than conferring skills. Even in cases where this is true, schooling is performing a vital function by mitigating a market imperfection (that is, the poor information that employers would otherwise have about worker abilities) education adopted new higher-yielding technologies faster than did less well-educated farmers. And some of the benefits from their education spilled over to others: once the 'early adopters' had demonstrated the value of the new technologies, their success encouraged other farmers to switch to the more productive crops.

Better education for youngsters also results in better health later in life. This in turn improves his or her overall well-being, and also increases their subsequent productivity, making higher wages or non-wage earnings likely. Furthermore, the quality of a person's education can affect the health and nutrition of his or her children. This is especially true in the case of mothers. Child health is found to be related systematically to the level of education of the mother.

At the macro-economic level, the evidence suggests that improving educational quantity and quality does lead to more rapid economic growth and thus a more prosperous society. Most of the empirical research to date has used quantitative measures of education - enrolment rates in the early studies, then more recently measures of the stock of human capital embodied in the labour force.

Education can enhance social development by transmitting shared values, beliefs, and traditions. This 'citizenship education' is the bedrock of many educational systems, although systems that are more decentralised and based on models of autonomy, this aspect of the educational system may become diluted. Finally, education enriches lives directly through the pleasure of intelligent thought and the sense of empowerment that it gives students.

Economists too often overlook this 'consumption' aspect of education, and prefer to focus instead on the more quantifiable effects of education on productivity or aggregate growth. A study suggested that 32 countries will not achieve universal primary education. Furthermore, at least 44 countries will fall short of the gender equity goals, yet girls' education is even more important than that of boys.

Education For All conference in Senegal argues for a broader and deeper commitment to education for all. First, it calls not just for universal access to school, but universal completion of the primary cycle, with internationally competitive results in terms of student learning. And second, it recognises that Education for all (EFA) is one in which universal primary education is seen as but one of the many steps in education which developing countries need to take to become part of the 'knowledge economies'.

Secondary and higher education are also important components needed for a dynamic economy and for human development. There are also situations of conflicts and violence in many EFA countries, i.e., teachers murdered, schools destroyed, refugees and displaced children. Of the 32 countries at risk on EFA at least 11 are in conflict. The recent downturn in economic development worldwide, which has been aggravated by the September 11, 2001 terrorist attacks on the USA, will make it harder to achieve the Dakar goals for EFA. How elusive the promise of quality education for all is, can be illustrated with a number of points:

— Over 130 million children are out of school. Two thirds of them are girls, close to 1 billion are illiterate adults.

— Globally, one third of pupils drop out before they are functionally literate. In Bangladesh, 80 percent of those who complete grade 5 fail to achieve minimum competence in reading and mathematics.

— Out of school children are more likely to be girls and/or from poor families.

Much has been made recently of the EFA financing gap, that is to say, the difference between the amount of money countries are currently able to mobilise internally and externally, and the amount they will need for achieving universal primary coverage. Many EFA countries have recently begun to benefit from debt relief under the 1996 Heavily Indebted Poor Countries Initiative (HIPC). Debt relief from the Bank's concessional lending agency, the International Development Association or IDA, will alone average some US$375 million per year over the next 8 years. Average social sector spending will increase from 5.8 percent of GDP to 7.0 per cent of GDP. It is clear that the HIPC debt relief initiative will give many countries a much-needed window of opportunity as regards EFA, but much more will still need to be done.

Education systems in many of your countries have been obliged to run on extremely short school years, with primary school children putting in 500 to 700 hours per year, shortened even further by industrial action. This comes at a time when these systems need to be playing catch-up with international systems in which students are spending literally twice as much time in school each year, from 1000 to over 1200 hours a year in most developed countries.

Important progress can be made, and the World Bank and other partners are prepared to invest as never before in the EFA effort. The effort to fill the financing gap must necessarily be matched by a firm commitment at the country level to fill the policy gap. Such a partnership will place the EFA movement on a much firmer footing. 'Good' education policy is embedded in good macro-economic policy, creating a stable economy with predictable tax revenues which can sustain the public expenditures for education.

The World Bank as well as European Union Governments, have often been lambasted for their insistence on creating that environment, by means of sound monetary policy which keeps inflation low, and by means of a responsible government budget where debt financing is limited. 'Good' education policy is also based on proper 'delivery' of education, ensuring that teachers on the payroll turn up and indeed teach, and that school budgets arrive at the school intact and are not siphoned off.

Countries can take decisive policy steps to improve the educational access and attainment of students from poorer families. Sometimes the reforms are intended to increase the magnitude and effectiveness of public spending on such students, as was the case.in Uganda; in other cases, as in El Salvador, reforms simply made it easier for households to subsidise the education of their children. Let me say a few words about each of these examples.

In 1997, Uganda's President Museveni made an election pledge to provide free primary education to all. Up until that point, education had not appeared as a government priority and the sudden shift was perhaps due to short-term political considerations. More likely though, it reflected Uganda's recognition of education as an important aspect of human development as well as an investment in its future. The economic recovery paved the way for committing the resources necessary for such a substantial undertaking.

After being elected, President Museveni followed through on his promise, waiving enrolment fees, abolishing parent association fees, and creating a climate where all parents expected an affordable place for their children in school. The response was overwhelming: enrolment rates skyrocketed (a doubling of official enrolments, although these may overstate the true change). Children who were previously excluded from school - those from poor families, those with uneducated parents, and girls - are now enrolled, and primary enrolment is nearly universal. This increase is truly remarkable, though it should come as no surprise that there are still problems.

Public financing is an issue of course, although a simultaneous effort to enhance the transparency of public funds for education has dramatically increased the percentage of funds that actually make it to schools. Sustainability is another issue, and the experience of Tanzania is cautionary: in that country, primary enrolment rates rose tremendously in the 1970s but today are slipping.

El Salvador in 1991 took a very different tack to increasing percentage of children in school - especially in rural areas.4 Building on a community-based model that developed after its long-running civil war, the EDUCO program formalised and expanded this educational system in rural areas with schools managed autonomously by community education associations. The Ministry of Education contracts with these associations to deliver a given curriculum to an agreed number of students in exchange for a specific budget. The associations are then responsible for hiring and firing teachers, monitoring teacher performance, and equipping and maintaining schools.

Initial evidence suggests that the program has played a substantial role in increasing enrolment, lowering absences and lowering dropout rates. Perhaps surprisingly, although the expansion of rural schools through the EDUCO program was rapid, it did not result in lower achievement test scores. A large part of maintaining quality has been attributed to the increased community involvement that this schooling model engenders. The education content of a country is firmly rooted in the culture. Similarly, the active ingredients of its education system, like the organisation of primary, secondary, and higher education, as well as the division of labour between general and vocational education, are to a large extent determined by historical development.

Yet, these national characteristics of education systems do not preclude international learning. Those responsible for decisions on the education system can learn a great deal from the wealth of international experiences with the organisation of education in a system. The 'good practice' in the organisation of educational systems will generally point to empowering the professionals, the teachers and the principals.

School autonomy or 'decentralisation' is frequently used as a term to denote those systems with a large responsibility vested in the professional community of the education system. The term 'autonomous' should not be taken to mean a lack of accountability; responsibility cannot survive without accountability and transparency. Transparency of the results of schools (preferably in terms of value added, i.e. correcting for differences in the entry level of children in the school) is a relatively new phenomenon in the education world, but it is quickly taking hold in many countries.

Parents and communities are eager to know whether 'their' school is living up to expectations, and hence they welcome the comparisons. Once schools have full professional autonomy and are transparent in their performance, parental pressure on schools and parental choice between schools may create a further incentive for the school's professional community to reach for the best possible quality. None of these notions of good practice is easily achieved, as all require extensive and also inclusive debate and small steps in education policy. These notions should not be seen as a rigid framework, but have translations in different countries in very different forms. Such measures taken during the East Asia crisis (in particular in Indonesia) show that such targeting is not only a gain to the poor, but to society as a whole.

Basic principles for effective development cooperation are:

— Ownership of education reform in the country: Reform cannot be 'bought,' it needs the participation and support of a broad array of stakeholders, at both the local and national level, from policymakers to teachers to community groups for it to take root and flower. If there is no broad ownership, then the chances of successful implementation will be remote indeed.

— Education cooperation is first and foremost exchange of knowledge and experience.

— Substantial general budget support for education becomes a winning proposition if the policy environment is 'right'.

— In the absence of good policies the emphasis should be on 'creating room for momentum' towards good policies.

Upgrading and expanding the local capacity of ministries, of think tanks, of civil society, of decentralised education units, of statistical agencies is an essential element of education cooperation. Civil service reform should be designed so as to keep qualified people in the country, not to push them out. Substantial additional resources are required to promote EFA and even more for an overall upgrade of education in developing countries.

Defining the resources needs under 'good policies' plus the requirements for engagement with countries with moderate or poor policies. The international community must not think of itself as a neutral bystander in all this. If poverty reduction is a global public good, and if illiteracy is a persistent element of, and contributor to, poverty, then we have a responsibility to work together in support of developing-country governments that are willing to attack the problem.

One role for the international community is to support the development of such benchmarking information, as well as its use by developing countries. For example, donors may need to help sponsor the design of tests that are appropriate not only for the developed world, where the largest market may exist, but also for the developing world. And to encourage poor countries to make their educational performance more transparent, donors should be willing, at least initially, to assume some of the costs of implementing the tests.

Countries that are pinned down by excessive debt burdens may understandably lack the strength and manoeuvrability to implement poverty-targeted reforms of their educational systems. Debt relief is one way to augment for a country's long-run capacity to increase access to quality education. There may be also international debate on other ways to provide long-run finance, if that is the major roadblock to achieve universal primary quality education.

In which the international community can help is by informing developing country governments and other stakeholders about the successes and failures of education reform in other countries. World Bank, try to do this in several ways. First, their educational project teams draw on their own considerable cross-country experience, as well as the experience from their colleagues and other experts that has been codified through the Bank's knowledge management system. Second, the Bank both carries out and sponsors research, in order to turn 'good practice' anecdotes into generalisable lessons about what works and under what circumstances.

Third, the Bank organises and provides inputs to seminars for policymakers and others in developing countries; one of the most useful tools is peer learning, in which they help connect participants with their peers from other developing countries who have already designed and implemented similar reforms. As in the case of benchmarks, there is a public-good nature to some of these services, implying that they will tend to be under-supplied by the market.

Cross-agency coordination is easier to launch reforms if a country's entire education-related efforts are working in the same direction, rather than being dissipated in a thousand different directions. It is important to coordinate well, both within the government and among its partners in the donor community. Within the government, the country needs to ensure that efforts in one area are complemented by efforts in another.

This is one of the core insights guiding the Comprehensive Development Framework approach that the Bank has adopted over the past two years. Efforts to expand educational access by building schools may be blocked by shortcomings in other sectors - road problems that keep students from getting to school, civil-service procedures that encourage corruption or absenteeism among teachers, or macroeconomic conditions that require children to work full-time to support their families.

School reform is a perennial issue in American education. At the turn of the 20th century, John Dewey provided reasons to be concerned with educational improvement, two of which continue to stand out at the dawn of the 21st century-furthering democratic ideals through a broadly educated citizenry, and obtaining a viable economic future for all citizens. Formal education is society's best available route to assure citizens' participation in the world of work.

The relationship between education and income has never been stronger than in the closing years of the 20th century. By contrast, today's young male high school dropout not only earns less than half as much as the average high school dropout of 25 years ago (in inflation-adjusted dollars), he actually earns less, in constant dollars, than did young high school dropouts of 1949, a half-century ago.

In the emerging world information economy described by Friedman, there is an increasing premium for obtaining further formal education. The U.S. Department of Labor notes that the education level expected to see the most rapid growth in job prospects over the next 10 years is the associate degree, followed by the bachelor's, doctoral, and master's degrees. All jobs requiring less than an associate degree are expected to have lower percentage increases in job growth. The clear conclusion of the work of the U.S. Department of Labor is this: "Education is essential in getting a high-paying job".

In US, the National Assessment of Educational Progress (NAEP) provides data in several of these areas, including reading, mathematics, and science. Whereas large sample sizes make it possible to find statistical significances among the various trends at different points in time, all nine of the trends have in fact been stable over the past 30 years.

Dropout and achievement problems is to gain an understanding of the factors that contribute to school failure. A variety of studies have indicated that poverty, minority status, parents' educational attainment, and other variables beyond the control of students have tended to lead to low achievement and failure to thrive in schooling. Nora and Rendon found that even among those at-risk students who successfully complete high school, community college completion rates are low. The number of students in these categories is expected to rise in comparison to White, middle-class, native English speakers whose parents attended college.

"Risk factors" in education commonly refer to situations or characteristics that may have an impact on the likelihood that a student will graduate from high school. Although the U.S. Department of Education's National Center for Educational Statistics (NCES) has been unsuccessful in its efforts to get 50 states to agree on a common definition of "dropout".

A large number of variables have been shown to correlate with dropping out of school. However, with the exception of the variable, "attending a very high-poverty, non-selective urban high school", no combination of these has been shown to be strongly predictive of dropping out. Many students encountering these variables, even several at one time, are able to successfully complete both high school and college. Therefore, it is important to note at the outset that no one correlate, or set of correlates, necessarily destines a child or group of children to failure.

A large number of variables have been found to be associated with individual-level risk of educational failure: Natriello et al. noted that limited English proficiency was a significant risk factor. Stevens and Price listed prenatal drug and alcohol exposure, premature birth, HIV infection, lead poisoning, and the experience of abuse and homelessness as significant risk factors. Dynarski and Gleason conducted an extensive review of research on "risk" and added the following student-level variables: student has an external locus of control; low self-esteem; is not "very sure" of graduating from high school; has one or more children; was absent 20 or more times per year; is more than one year behind in school; received low grades; has had disciplinary problems at school; has attended five or more schools; spends less than an hour per week on homework; and spends no time reading for fun.

A significant problem identified in the Dynarski and Gleason research is that, in spite of having data available on a total of 18 student-level variables, and being able to combine those into four composite risk variables, the authors were unable to produce a student-level composite variable that could predict later dropout behavior with near 50% accuracy, and very often incorrectly identified as likely dropouts students who, in fact, graduated from high school. The presence of high rates of both "false positives" (students statistically identified as likely to drop out who in fact go on to graduate on schedule) and "false negatives" (a failure to correctly target other students as likely to drop out who do, in fact, drop out) is a serious limitation of current student-level risk identification programs.

Race/ethnicity is a special case. Race is a complex variable for the purposes of categorization of risk factors. Being African American or Hispanic increases one's statistical chances of dropping out of school; however, some of the reasons for these statistical changes may operate at an individual level, others at a family level, others at a school level, and still others at a community/societal level. Regardless of the level at which it is discussed, the fact remains that minority students are much less likely to thrive in public schools.

Campbell et al., for example, found that on the 1998 National Assessment of Educational Progress (NAEP), African American students scored 28-32 points lower than White students, and Hispanic students scored 22-26 points lower than White students. Natriello et al. identified poverty, mother's education, and family composition as family-level indicators of risk. Mothers' education level has been found to be a consistent predictor of students' failure to thrive in public education.Parents who themselves lack a high school education may not be as prepared to help their children complete their homework or navigate the experience of secondary school.

In addition, immigrant parents often do not understand the U.S. schooling system, and may not be aware of opportunities available to improve their children's achievement. More studies focus on mothers' education levels, as opposed to fathers' education levels, in part because in the case of single-parent families, the child is more likely to live with the mother. On average, students living in single-parent families do less well on standardized tests.

Furthermore, students from single-parent families are more than twice as likely to drop out of school as students living in two-parent families. This is in part because single-parent family status tends to be associated with other "risk-related" variables such as poverty and minority status. Over a quarter of U.S. children under the age of 18 live in single-parent families, with over 80% of these living with their mothers.

Poverty concentration, class size, and school size are all associated with lower rates of academic success. U.S. Department of Education analyses of 1996 NAEP data indicate that, on average, nine-year-old children attending schools in which 75+% of students received free or reduced-price lunch scored 37 points lower in reading and 21 points lower in mathematics than nine-year-old students attending schools with 25% or lower free or reduced-price lunch.

Balfanz and Legters examined the characteristics of high schools from which less than half of all students graduated. The most unifying of all relatively common characteristics was very high school-level rates of poverty.

School location is a significant predictor of students' probability of thriving in school. Grissmer found that, regardless of section of the country, attending an urban school negatively affected a student's probability of academic success. Balfanz and Legters found that virtually all of the U.S. high schools with less than a 50% graduation rate were located in inner-city districts. The reasons are fairly well-known: inner-city schools tend to have less prepared teachers and less funding than their suburban counterparts.

In addition, Grissmer found that, all other things being equal, students attending schools located in the Northeastern and North-Central states outperformed students in the Southeastern and Western states. In short, there are student-, family-, school-, and community-level risk factors of school failure. In general, students who have been exposed to such clear risk-inducing conditions as suffering from low self-esteem, coming from high-poverty backgrounds, being members of racial/ethnic minorities, whose parents are poorly educated, and who attend large schools with large classes in high-poverty, inner-city contexts are more likely to do poorly in school.

In US, the current school reform movement can be traced to the release of a series of commission reports during the 1980s and early 1990s that decried a "rising tide of mediocrity" in American schooling. The various commissions indicated that the nation was in danger of losing ground economically to other developed countries. They enumerated specific skills that employers claimed to be looking for in workers, which included not only basic skills, but also so-called "soft skills", such as reliability and a positive attitude.

Many of the reports recommended school reform that set tougher standards and focused on the acquisition of basic skills. As a result, education reform became defined in some circles as raising standards and increasing graduation requirements. Traditional academic skill improvement was the clear goal. These reforms of the late 1980s neither improved student test scores, nor increased high school graduation rates. Furthermore, the extra time devoted to academic courses took time away from student electives, often including vocational education.

In fact, vocational education had remained peripheral to the national debate. But during this time, many members of the vocational education community were rethinking their mission. Historically, the vocational track had tended to be sparse in academics, and the business community began to complain that students were coming to them without being fully prepared for work. The Grant Foundation report, together with other events, prompted school reform that had workforce preparation as a focus, including improving school-to-work transitions and a focus on obtaining postsecondary education as a preparation for careers.

So both the broader secondary education community, and the vocational education community within it, were rethinking their roles and structures at the same time. This provided an opportunity for dynamic intersections that integrated academic rigor with preparation for work for all students.

Vocational programs are changing. They may be attracting higher-achieving students who recognize the value of the kinds of introduction to careers that many career and technical programs offer. Vocational education as a part of public schooling began in the U.S. in the 19th century. Previously, public secondary schools had been designed to serve a small percentage of students completing elementary school. Most children were expected to learn a trade in the traditional apprentice fashion, by the side of a family member, farmer, or craftsman.

When compulsory schooling extended into the teen years, students began to be sorted by likely outcomes. The sorting itself tended to ensure a "practical" (i.e., local economy directed) education for the great majority of students, and effectively ensured the marginalization of vocational education. Historically, vocational education programs tended to include those students who were at risk of not finishing high school. They were students whom counselors and other adults assumed would not go on to any postsecondary education. These students were provided with vocational education so that they could earn a decent living after leaving school.

Although vocational education in the U.S. did not enjoy high status, it did prepare generations of young people for the work roles that awaited them in factories, farms, and offices. Vocational education succeeded at this mission as long as there were enough jobs in these areas, but such a use of secondary education has become problematic. Since the end of the 1980s, the globalization of the economy has had an increasing impact on the American economy.

Between 1970 and 1993, the proportion of U.S. workers employed in manufacturing fell 41%, down to only 16% of the total workers employed. This has happened in many sectors, from steel and automobiles to household goods and apparel. The old expectation that a young person could get a job in the plant where one's father had worked no longer held. In fact, many fathers were unable to keep those jobs themselves. During the 1980s and 1990s, vocational education enrollments declined in traditional vocational content areas-business, agriculture, and the trades.

The vocational education community began to feel the pressure to adapt or risk becoming irrelevant in the 21st century economy. Most of the traditional areas needed to be infused with new technologies-computerized diagnostics in auto repair, numerically controlled machines in machine shops, and high-tech equipment in health occupations classes. Clearly, for those changes to happen, staff would need professional development on these new technologies as well.

High schools needed to provide a more expansive academic and vocational curriculum premised upon broad career clusters, rather than preparation for particular jobs. Such programs needed to become better linked to postsecondary occupational education, which, in turn, could provide greater specificity and more direct application to immediate employment. These programs could also point to further postsecondary education and workplace training opportunities over a lifetime.

To reflect this change in philosophy and the kinds of programs offered, in 1998, the American Vocational Association changed its name to the Association for Career and Technical Education. The new ACTE urged its members to use the term "career and technical education" (CTE) in place of "vocational education". The most important changes were a focus on increasing the academic skills of CTE students, on trying to erase the stigma attached to vocational education, and on having all students meet the higher standards that had become prevalent. The goal of CTE became for all students to finish high school prepared to either enter the workplace, or to go on to postsecondary education.

This broader mission challenged vocational educators to teach beyond the confines of specific occupations, and instead to prepare students for a more demanding world of work. Stone summarized this expanded view of CTE in which students are prepared for the contemporary workplace along three non-exclusive vectors: education that uses work as a context for developing broader general skills, education that uses work as a context for developing more widely recognized skills required for long-term occupational and career success, and, education that uses work as a context for developing occupationally specific skills.

These can be referred to as education through work, education about work, and education for work. All students should have the opportunity to learn school subjects with work as the context of their learning. Communities abound with work/learning opportunities, and these have power to transform the entire curriculum. In this way, all teachers in elementary and secondary school can become involved in career and technical education. Education through work and occupations draws upon the work of cognitive scientists who provide evidence that practical pursuits can be an important context for academic learning.

Career and technical education can teach about work. Education about work, like education through work, is meant to be broadly educational. The curriculum assumes that career and technical knowledge-knowledge about the world of work-is valid school knowledge, good in its own right, and rightfully belongs in the common core of knowledge that all students should possess. Workplaces are a primary site of the construction of culture, since people spend so much of their lives at work. Thus, what transpires in the workplace constitutes content worthy of a place in the school curriculum.

All students need to learn about social aspects of work, such as democratic rights in the workplace, safety, and the prospect of race or gender discrimination. They need to know about career ladders, labor markets, job-seeking skills, and job-keeping skills. They need to understand firsthand why some jobs are considered "better" than others. They need to understand how to effectively allocate resources, acquire and use information, develop solid interpersonal skills, use and troubleshoot technology, and work with and modify systems used in business and industry.

All teachers, but particularly specialist career and technical education teachers, can be involved in this aspect of the subject. There is much room here for collaboration between academic and vocational teachers. Classrooms and laboratories in schools and colleges are well-suited to provide education about work, whereas partnerships with actual work sites would be the ideal way to provide education about work.

Education for jobs in the economy is a vital aspect of career and technical education. Although many argue that preparation for jobs should probably be concentrated in the postsecondary phase of students' lives (e.g., in community and technical colleges), there are many students who are developmentally ready to prepare for occupations at earlier ages. Programs for these students, often located in regional vocational centers, must meet the two goals of rigorous academic development and rigorous career development. These programs must also link to postsecondary education and training opportunities.

For most young people, however, secondary schools should provide high-quality career guidance services and competence in communication, numeracy, literacy, and computer abilities, all of which lead to more specific preparation at the postsecondary level. Much of what occurs in U.S. high schools is shaped by state laws and local programs. However, since the passage of the Smith-Hughes Act in 1917, the Federal government has been involved in the provision of vocational education to U.S. youth in high schools. As the commissions cited above issued their critiques on the state of U.S. education in the 1980s, the U.S. Congress responded in the reauthorizations of its vocational education laws. Congress' reauthorizations encouraged reforms of vocational education to make a clearer transition to postsecondary education, to infuse more academic rigor, to include more work-related experiences, and to make vocational education more accountable.

In 1990, the Carl D. Perkins Vocational and Applied Technology Education Act mandated that Federally funded vocational education programs institute several reforms. These included the following:

1. the development of tech prep programs;
2. the integration of vocational and academic curricula;
3. the promotion of work-related experience; and
4. accountability as a required element of funding.

By the mid-1990s, tech prep systems had been implemented in over half of the comprehensive high schools and the majority of community colleges in the U.S.

Several studies have addressed this implementation process; however, none of the studies include student outcomes. Bragg began a longitudinal study in 1998 of eight tech prep consortia that were considered "mature implementers." Due to large differences in implementation across sites, she did not aggregate results over the eight consortia, but rather described the ranges of outcomes.

For schools to fulfill their societal mission, Resnick concluded, they must focus on those aspects of learning that occur in out-of-school learning situations, and include those aspects that could be replicated within the school curriculum. Proponents of curriculum integration stated that it could serve several important purposes. First, it could reform secondary education for at-risk students and others not in the academic track, making it more rigorous and inclusive of the kinds of competencies perceived to be lacking in traditional vocational (and general) tracks.

When curriculum integration was coupled with new organizational structures, it formed part of what became known as the new vocationalism, which referred to a broadening of the goals of vocational education beyond job-specific training. But beyond this, curriculum integration could bring with it the opportunity to change the entire high school. Teachers could collaborate with peers outside of their discipline, and students would be provided with engaging academic courses that were related to broader themes of adult life or careers.

Pedagogy, too, could change, as academic courses presenting students with applications of traditional bodies of knowledge, and vocational teachers incorporating rigorous methods and deeper understanding of various technologies. Indeed, formal and informal tracks themselves could become obsolete, as students oriented around career themes, regardless of their next step. Lofty goals are rarely realized quickly, and the 1994 National Assessment of Vocational Education (NAVE) found that integration was moving forward slowly. NAVE researchers found that teachers did not have enough time to work on curriculum integration, both academic and vocational teachers resisted the idea, and a larger framework within which integration could take place was lacking.

There were many ways to integrate academic and vocational curricula, some of which incorporated few, if any, innovative elements. For instance, where vocational teachers were simply incorporating more academics into their otherwise unchanged classes in an unchanged high school, or purchasing off-the-shelf curricular materials, teacher collaboration and engagement with integration was minimal.

Other barriers to curriculum integration included both high school graduation and college admission requirements that often did not recognize or grant credit for integrated courses. The NAVE report noted that integration was furthest along in those states and districts that were undertaking other comprehensive education reforms that included the workforce preparation of all students. The NAVE report recommended the further emphasis of integration in vocational legislation.

Like many proposed changes to the structure of schooling, the initiative to integrate academic and vocational education has been supported with only anecdotal evidence of increased student engagement and achievement. To date, it has been difficult to assess the effectiveness of integration for all students, and thus for any subset of the high school population, such as at-risk students. In addition to the paucity of studies on the effects of curriculum integration, "scaling up" this particular reform has proven challenging.

Successfully scaling up reforms is difficult under any circumstances. Given the relatively low status that vocational education has in high schools, and the fact that vocational and academic staff often interact little, much less collaborate, spreading reform based on curriculum integration has proven to be very slow. In co-op programs, students receive training in the context of a paid job. Students may also be involved in a school-based enterprise, an on-site work-related experience such as running the student store. Alternatively, they might be involved in off-site activities, such as building a house or producing other goods or services for sale.

Students enroll in related classes, and often decide how to use the income generated by the enterprise, but are usually not paid. Students have reported that working in school enterprises provided more opportunities for doing a range of tasks and for working in teams than was the case in their outside jobs. Students also reported having the space to make mistakes, whereas their outside jobs often did not have such opportunities. Combining school and work is usually beneficial in the lives of young people; most high school students want or need to work, and the effects on students of part-time work of less than 20 hours per week can be positive.

As students worked with each other over longer periods of time and across several courses, they made friendships with their classmates. Those relationships supported learning and completing assignments. Teachers also had the chance to know each student better. In some cases, teachers were required to telephone home if a student had been absent. This created for the students "a strong sense of adult involvement in their life at school, and close connections with a stable group of classmates who are seriously engaged in schoolwork"-all of which promoted staying in school and completing the program.

Many students begin to disengage from school in the middle school years. Schools that waited until the 11th grade to begin these programs found that many of the target students had already dropped out. Furthermore, schools found that their students were not qualified for substantive work-related experiences or internships in grade 11 or 12 if they had only had 1 year of preparation and introduction to the field. Beginning a program in grades 9 or 10 was found to better prepare students for their workrelated experiences. The Pauly et al. report concluded that the three main strategies needed to develop strong school-to-work programs and improve students' education were as follows:

1. change the nature and content of instruction to integrate academic and vocational education;
2. provide personalized student support for the increased academics and to foster a sense of belonging to a special community; and
3. provide work-based learning opportunities that show how curriculum content is used in the workplace.

As with curriculum integration, scaling up work-based learning opportunities presents a challenge. Only a finite number of workplaces exist, and only a subset of those will be willing and able to work with schools to provide slots for students. Firms that have not formed partnerships with schools, and firms in which their sole experience with young people is through individuals responding to classified ads, often have negative attitudes about youth.

However, many firms that provide structured work-based learning opportunities are pleased with the quality of the work done by young people.

School to Work Opportunities Act

At nearly the same time as the report by Pauly et al., the School to Work Opportunities Act (STWOA) was passed. Its goals were to encourage states to develop and implement comprehensive statewide systems to help all young people prepare for high-skill, high-wage careers, utilizing workplaces as learning environments. These new systems would provide students with career awareness and exploration, work-based learning opportunities, and school-based activities to connect the learning at school to that at work, while ensuring strong academics.

An early evaluation of school-to-work (STW) programs found promising practices, but did not draw definitive conclusions. Urquiola et al. also identified the kinds of work-based learning opportunities that STW programs provide-paid work experience, unpaid internships, service learning, job shadowing, and school-based enterprises. Many of these opportunities are provided under the auspices of other reform efforts and are not necessarily called STW or funded with STW money.

Hughes, Moore, and Bailey investigated the claim that work-based learning increases student motivation, and thus academic achievement. In the student internship programs they studied, they did not see much application or exploration of school-based knowledge such as reading, writing, or mathematics on the job. Rather than expecting internship sites to reinforce school-based knowledge, they suggested that programs could incorporate work-based situations into the classroom, and reinforce school-based knowledge through student internship experiences.

In a national evaluation, Hershey et al. found that within the three major elements of the STWOA-work-based learning experiences, school-based learning experiences, and connecting activities-career exploration activities (e.g., individual career plans) were the most prevalent school-based learning activities. STW partnerships seemed to be focusing on career awareness, rather than forcing students into narrowly defined occupations.

High Schools That Work (HSTW) began in 1987 as an initiative of the Southern Regional Education Board (SREB). It has since grown to include more than 1,100 schools in 26 states. Its goal is to "raise the academic achievement of career-bound high school students by combining the content of traditional college preparatory studies with vocational studies". This is accomplished through rigorous vocational courses, along with more required academic coursework.

Common planning time is provided for teachers to collaborate on curriculum integration, and higher standards and expectations are set for all students. Extra help is provided for students, as well as an individualized advising system. Finally, HSTW uses assessment information to improve student learning. All high school seniors who will complete a vocational or technical concentration at HSTW sites are required to participate in the HSTW Assessment, which is based on the National Assessment of Educational Progress (NAEP) tests of reading, mathematics, and science.

Research has shown that "HSTW students, including vocational students, take more academic courses than students at the same schools did" before HSTW was implemented. Schools that have implemented the design faithfully usually see improved student achievement and higher attendance, graduation, retention, and postsecondary attendance rates.

Career academies have existed since the 1970s, but their focus shifted in the late 1980s from a dropout-prevention strategy to an approach that can prepare all students for both work and postsecondary education. In a longitudinal study on outcomes for students in career academies, Kemple and Snipes reported a 15-fold increase in the number of career academies during the decade of the 1990s, with many more planned. Most career academies incorporate the main elements of what is known as "the new vocationalism"-a broad career focus, a link to business, and curriculum integration.

Kemple and Snipes noted the ways in which career academies differ from traditional vocational education, and reflect the new vocationalism, within a smaller learning community. They distinguish a career academy as an approach that:

1) is organized as a school within a school, where students stay with a group of teachers over three or four years;

2) offers students both academic and vocational curriculum, usually integrated around a career theme; and

3) has established partnerships with businesses in order to build connections between school and work.

Some high schools have been reorganized into career pathways, replacing traditional tracks such as college prep, vocational, and general tracks.A career pathway is a cluster of occupations that share similar interests and strengths, although they may differ in terms of length of education and training required. For example, a cluster such as engineering, manufacturing, and industrial technology can provide students with a broad introduction to many fields, such as machinist or engineer.

Career pathways form the context for integrated activities such as senior projects and other interdisciplinary activities. Pathways, like many other reforms with roots in vocational education, are intended to have strong connections with business and industry and with postsecondary education, in order to give students internships or other applied experiences. Pathways are also intended to provide a rigorous, coherent program of study that includes highlevel academics, in addition to technology applications and work-based learning.

The U.S. Department of Education has identified 16 career clusters that high schools can choose from in developing their pathways, depending on local labor market opportunities. The evidence from these high school organizational structures seems to indicate that career academies, magnets, and pathways are possibly productive ways for secondary vocational education to position itself for the future.

The elements of these structures are pedagogically and theoretically sound, and, in the case of magnets and academies, have proven effective in the best of cases. One possible reason is that they are strategies for all students, not low-status programs for those not deemed "college material." Students are very aware of their position in the high school hierarchy, and the stigma of vocational education may have grown strong enough in some schools to preclude it from being successful in its traditional forms.

Another reason is that career academies, magnets, and pathways restructure the school. In the best of cases, students feel that their teachers care, their peers care, and they all share a common interest and goal. The students are not the only ones involved in positive relationships; teachers, too, have developed professional communities around certain themes, and have become responsible to each other.

Perhaps non-career-related magnets experience the same results. However, it is useful to note that in reports to Crain et al, students claimed that their high school experience was useful in developing a career identity and in becoming proficient at something. Non-career-related high school reorganization along the lines of academies or magnets would be unlikely to produce this result.

4

Priorities of Educational Innovation

Education reform requires comprehensive approaches that are realistically planned in view of the capacity for innovation within local contexts. Educational, historical, political, socio-economic and cultural differences between countries make it difficult to predict the effects of proposed reforms on the basis of international experience in educational development. Furthermore, stakeholder views on priorities and approaches differ. Forging common ground between these diverging interests and ensuring ownership of the initiatives is a complex and demanding process.

Many common trends can be recognised in the field of international education development, such as the emphasis on life-long learning opportunities, learner-centred approaches, and the integration of ICT in education. The contexts in which trends are addressed differ widely, but the outcomes of policy initiatives tend to be similar: there is a wide gap between policy rethorics and concrete change in practice.

Although successful change can be accomplished at a small-scale, system-wide application is usually disappointing and sustained results are difficult to ascertain. Problems include huge innovation ambitions that are accompanied with too short timelines and too little investments, especially in teachers, lack of alignment between system components (teacher education, curriculum, assessment), and the lack of involvement of all relevant stakeholders.

The context for education development in developing countries, especially in Sub-Saharan Africa, includes a number of additional challenges such as pervasive poverty, inadequate financing for development, insufficient scientific knowledge, the lack of capacity in strategic planning and in research and development capability, extensive armed conflicts, high fertility and the HIV/AIDS pandemic. All these challenges form barriers to expanding access to and improving the quality of education.

Experiences with educational innovation have been mixed and often disappointing, as Lewin states: "the developing world is littered with educational reform proposals that either have not been seriously implemented or that were overtaken by events before their effects were transparent". Quality improvement in education is high on the agenda in many countries, but difficult choices have to be made. Countries need to invest in the entire education sector, using a broad sectoral approach for education development that is linked to sound macroeconomic policies.

Many countries are ready to move ahead, but will not be able to tackle the challenges alone. For the poorest developing countries the Heavily Indebted Poor

Countries (HIPC) initiative may offer some possibilities. This initiative was launched by the World Bank and the IMF in 1996, and aims to reduce the external debt of the poorest, most heavily indebted countries by placing debt relief within the framework for poverty reduction.

The challenge for the education sector in the HIPC countries will be to obtain some of the resources released by the initiative, and especially to use them in an efficient and equitable way. Effective reform is unlikely to succeed, however, unless government-led partnerships replace traditional, narrowly focused, externally driven aid programs. The challenge will be to manage donor contributions to maximum national advantage and to avoid the often occurring problem of a government driven education system existing next to a variety of donor driven projects that are only supplementing instead of strengthening the formal system.

The current emphasis therefore should be on sector-wide approaches in which governments and donors work in partnership, with the aim of fostering country ownership and developing sustainable strategies for educational development. Such a policy context offers new opportunities to develop more comprehensive and systemic reform approaches, and to organise external aid more effectively. It also, however, increases demands on national planning and implementation capacity at all levels in the education system, leading to new capacity building challenges and learning needs.

Verspoor outlines a number of priority objectives for education development in developing countries. These include:

a. *Universal primary education*: this is important to increase the educational attainment of the labour force. This priority is in line with the 1990 Jomtien World Conference on Education for All and the World Education Forum in Dakar (2000). Much work still has to be done in this area as in many developing countries the enrolment rates are still low, and many children (especially in rural areas) do not finish full primary education (UNESCO, 2000).

b. *Gradual expansion of access to the full education cycle*: policymakers should acknowledge the importance of secondary education. There is already a trend to expand this part of the education sector. Given the age group, youth in secondary education can also be cost-efficiently targeted for special interventions related to problems with HIV/AIDS, reproductive health, social attitudes, and civic values. Youth and adults who lack essential literacy and numeracy skills should get the opportunity to participate in adult education programs.

c. Enhancing vocational and technical skills of youth and adults through continuous job-related skill development programs offered by demand-driven systems, including public and private providers.

d. Strengthening post-primary science, mathematics and technology in secondary and post-secondary institutions so that a selected number of students are prepared especially for scientific and technological careers.

e. Revitalising national research and development programs.

Verspoor takes a rather economic perspective on the aims of education, when he refers to the importance of the educational attainment of the labour force, to the need for continuous job-related skill development programs and to preparation for scientific and technological careers. It is important that we realise that in every society education also serves other functions, such as personal development, and transfer of social, cultural and human values. Where we can agree with the priority objectives for education, the argumentation for most of them can be strengthened by referring to the other functions of education as well.

Every set of policy priorities should be guided by a clear vision on and reflection about 'what' to achieve through education and 'why', so as to make sure that in the end curricula reflect all relevant curriculum perspectives. With regard to the objective of achieving universal primary education it is important to emphasise that the focus should be solely on increasing access to formal primary education. The large number of drop-outs and early school-leavers, the needs of traumatised, sick and undernourished children as well as the expected contribution of education to poverty eradication should lead to a broad vision on education for all.

The heterogeneity of these factors and of backgrounds of potential learners implies that one cannot speak of one form or type of universal primary education for all. Dependent on their situation (including age, geographical and social circumstances) people should have an opportunity to choose from a number of options.

A wider approach should also encompass alternative strategies to reach out to the large number of drop-outs and school-leavers, to provide them with opportunities to develop lifelong learning and vocational skills, and to create equal opportunities for all to benefit. In such a broad vision the school should not be the only framework for providing quality education. Institutions and agencies for community development should also have a role, especially for adults in need of education.

Today, everywhere Governments have been embarking on substantial programs of reform in an attempt to develop more effective school systems and raise levels of student learning and achievement. It is however curious that countries and educational systems with very different political cultures and stages of economic development should all be pursuing what is to all appearances a very similar policy agenda.

In particular, there are a number of paradoxes and challenges in the application of principles and strategies from a developed to a developing educational context. In this respect, the Aga Khan East African school improvement initiative provides a unique insight into a sustained effort to build school improvement capacity and enhance student learning and attainment in a developing educational context.

Anderson claims that there are 'six key principles that taken together will enhance 'the chances for improving the quality of teaching and learning in schools':

— School based;

— Whole school as unit of change;

— On-going professional development of teachers;

— Attend to school management and other organisational conditions;

— Prepare for institutionalisation and sustainability;

— Involve stakeholders.

These principles form part of the conventional wisdom of school improvement in developed educational systems. What of course is more problematic is how these principles play-out in contexts radically different from those where they were derived. There are many terms and phrases in education that generate passionate support, but in practice lack operational clarity. Child-centred learning is one of these terms. This is not to say that the program originators are not clear about the concept, the difficulties occur as the concept is translated into practice.

There appear to be two ways in which this essentially Western educational term is used. First child-centred learning most usually refers either to a particular ethos within a school or classroom that prizes the individuality of the learner, that respects the current phase of their learning history, and that creates conditions within the school and classroom where the learner feels accepted and secure.

In simple terms this approach to child-centred learning refers to a caring, accepting and happy school environment. Another way of viewing child-centred learning is more technical and precise in so far as it relates to cognitive development. This approach works within the broad parameters of developmental psychology and consequently views the child as being an active learner and the teacher as the one who promotes learning skill and capability.

The aim of the teacher working within this tradition is to develop powerful learners who can respond successfully to the tasks that they are set, as well as the tasks they set themselves. The key point is that within whatever context learning takes place, it involves an 'active construction of meaning.'

Unfortunately securing child-.centred learning of the second type is not simply achieved by more or better training. There appear to be at least two formidable challenges to be met if authentic child-centred learning is to be achieved. One of the threats to child-centred learning is the narrowing of the definition of effective student learning to the point where it is equated with a range of test scores, rather than something broader.

The emphasis on test score focused target setting in many educational systems puts pressure on schools and on teachers to raise levels of achievement in the short term, by means of tactical responses such as homework clubs or teaching to the test. This leads to an impoverished interpretation of what constitutes learning. The first challenge, therefore, is to address this normative and politically attractive view of attainment and learning. It is evident from the case studies that teachers in Uganda, Kenya, and Tanzania are subject to significant expectations and pressure to ensure student success on national examinations.

Any changes in teaching and learning strategies that do not yield demonstrable short term improvements in student outcomes according to local accountability standards are unlikely to be fully implemented and sustained. This provides a difficult challenge for child-centred teaching methods given the predictable implementation dip experienced by teachers in the process of classroom change.

Promoters of educational change often focus their efforts on helping teachers modify their beliefs and classroom practices, but neglect the fact that many changes that teachers aspire to introduce in the classroom also require changes in student beliefs and approaches to learning. The Aga Khan projects give little attention to the important role of students in the process of classroom change.

Pedagogic versus Curriculum

Advocates of 'child-centred learning' often also argue persuasively for 'school based curriculum development' as providing a more authentic framework for student learning. The experience of successful contemporary school improvement efforts is that learning potential is best realised, and learning capability enhanced, through the.range of teaching and learning models that the teacher uses with her students. It is the deliberate use of a range of teaching and learning strategies that are rich in meta-cognitive content that delivers on both learning and achievement. But as has already been stressed, the teaching and learning strategies are not 'free-floating', but embedded in the schemes of work and curriculum content that teachers use to structure the learning in their lessons.

These schemes of work also have the potential to be shared between schools and to be made available for wider dissemination. As we will see, this way of working assumes a whole school dimension through: the staff development infrastructure the school has established; the emphasis on high expectations; the careful attention to consistency of teaching practice; and the discussion of pedagogy that pervades the cultures of these schools. By way of contrast, much recent centralised reform places great faith in the ability of curriculum guidelines to codify and ensure consistency of practice.

National governments now almost without exception outline curriculum guidelines, but require teachers to develop the detailed schemes of work involved and to select the most appropriate instructional strategies. Although guidelines ensure a degree of uniformity in the curriculum diet of students, it will not necessarily raise standards of performance.

There are three key implications for policy here. The first is that educational programmes need to be sufficiently comprehensive so that they link together in explicit and concrete ways curriculum content and teaching strategies. The second is that as Crandall and his colleagues have noted, 'it should not be assumed that involving teachers in developing innovations will invariably lead to better programmes,' 'the crucial variable is whether programs are implementable and attractive to teachers'. This leads to the third implication, the need to increase the number of comprehensive, school-wide models for school improvement that have been carefully developed and can be broadly disseminated.

The learning focus is the key to effective school improvement. This can only be achieved by linking together teaching and learning strategies within a curriculum context.

Professional Development and Leadership Training

The realisation of child-centred learning and appropriate curriculum support is not achievable without a strong focus on teacher learning and professional development. The commitment to teacher learning and professional development is a strong feature of the Aga Khan school improvement projects. It is clear that deliberate and focussed efforts were made in every case to enhance teacher learning.

The 'new professionalism' proposed by David Hargreaves suggest that paradoxically, many of the recent educational reform efforts are having the unintended consequence of eroding the traditional culture of individualism in teaching by forcing structural changes that are generating new forms of collaboration. The 'new professionalism' implies a change in the values and practices of teachers as structural changes are encouraging a move from 'individualism to collaboration' and from 'hierarchies to teams'.

In making his argument, Hargreaves sets out two propositions about the relationship between teacher and school development. The first is that there is little school development without teacher development. The second is that there is little teacher development without school development. The truth of the first proposition is axiomatic. The second is more controversial. What is particularly significant about contemporary school improvement strategies is that they both not only focus directly on improving student behaviour, learning and attainment, but also pay attention to teacher and school development.

There is now a significant amount of evidence to suggest that a school improvement strategy is more likely to advance achievement for all students if it addresses not only the learning of individual teachers, but also other dimensions of the organisational capacity of the school. This is now often referred to as school capacity. Without an emphasis on capacity a school will be unable to 'transform' itself or sustain continuous improvement efforts that result in student attainment.

Newmann, King and Young argue that professional development is more likely to advance achievement for all students in a school if it addresses not only the learning of individual teachers, but also other dimensions of the organisational capacity of the school. They define school capacity as the collective competency of the school as an entity to bring about effective change. They suggest that there are four core components of capacity:

— Knowledge, skills and dispositions of individual staff members;

— A professional learning community in which staff work collaboratively to set clear goals for student learning, assess how well students are doing, develop action plans to increase student achievement, whilst being engaged in inquiry and problem-solving;

— Program coherence which refers to the extent to which the school's programs for student and staff learning are co-ordinated, focussed on clear learning goals and sustained over a period of time;

— Technical resources - high quality curriculum, instructional material, assessment instruments, technology, workspace, etc.

If these ideas are to impact on practice, then it is critical to be able to define 'capacity' in operational terms. The 'conditions' have to be worked on at the same.time as the curriculum or other priorities the school has set itself. Conditions are the internal features of the school, the 'arrangements' that enable it to get work done. The 'conditions' within the school that are associated with a capacity for sustained improvement are:

— a commitment to staff development and the establishing of a professional learning community;

— practical efforts to involve staff, students and the community in school policies and decisions;

— 'transformational' leadership approaches that are both instructionally focused and dispersed amongst staff within the school;

— effective coordination strategies that ensure whole school consistency of practice and high expectations;

— serious attention to the potential benefits of enquiry and reflection and that gathers data on both achievement and learning;

— a commitment to collaborative planning activity that adapts external change for internal purposes.

Another aspect to building capacity is reflected in the networks that are established to support innovative work between schools. There has recently been much international interest in the role of networks in supporting school improvement. There are however various interpretations of the network concept. Although networks bring together those with like minded interests, they are more than just opportunities to share 'good practice'.

In education, networks promote the dissemination of good practice, enhance the professional development of teachers, support capacity building in schools, mediate between centralised and decentralised structures, and assist in the process of re-structuring and re-culturing educational organisations and systems. The qualities exhibited by such networks are however not easily acquired. A number of key conditions need to be in place if networks are to realise their potential as agents of educational innovation. In terms of school improvement, a number of conditions for effective networks can be identified:

— *Consistency of values and focus*: it is important that networks have a common aim and purpose, and that the values underpinning the network are well articulated.and 'owned' by those involved. This consistency of values and purpose also relates to the need for the focus of the network to be consistent with the overarching policy framework.

— *Clarity of structure*: effective networks are well organised with clear operating procedures and mechanisms for ensuring that maximum participation is achieved within and between schools. These structures promote involvement that is broad based, preferably with a whole organisation or systemic focus, rather than being narrow, limiting or particular.

— *Knowledge creation, utilisation and transfer*: the key purpose of networks is to create and disseminate knowledge to support educational improvement and innovation. Such knowledge and practice needs to be based on evidence, focus on the core features of schooling, and are subject to robust quality assurance procedures.

— *Rewards related to learning*: those who belong to networks need to feel that their involvement is worthwhile. Rewards for networking are best related to supporting professional development and the encouraging of learning.

— *Dispersed leadership and empowerment*: highly effective networks contain skilful people who collaborate and work well together. The skills required by network members are similar to the skill sets associated with effective teams and include a focus on dispersed leadership and empowerment.

— *Adequate resources*: networks need to be adequately resourced particularly in terms of time, finance and human capital. It is not necessarily the quantum of resources that is important, more crucially there needs to be flexibility in the way in which it is deployed.

Accordingly, networks need to be regarded as support structures for innovative schools, not only in disseminating 'good practice', but also in overcoming the traditional isolation of schools, and to a certain extent even challenging traditional hierarchical system structures. Such isolation may have been appropriate during times of stability, but during times of change there is a need to 'tighten the loose coupling', to increase collaboration and to establish more fluid and responsive structures.

In short, networks have the potential to support educational innovation and change by:

— Providing a focal point for the dissemination of good practice, the generalisability of innovation and the creation of 'action oriented' knowledge about effective educational practices.

— Keeping the focus on the core purposes of schooling in particular in creating and sustaining a discourse on teaching and learning.

— Enhancing the skill of teachers, leaders and other educators in change agent skills and managing the change process.

— Building capacity for continuous improvement at the local level, and in particular in creating professional learning communities, within and between schools.

Ensuring that systems of pressure and support are integrated not segmented. For example, professional learning communities incorporate pressure and support in a seamless way. Acting as a link between the centralised and decentralised schism resulting from many contemporary policy initiatives.

Sustainability is a broad concept that covers a range of issues related to the institutionalisation or embedding of change. The term embraces both human and material resources. There are a number of issues to do with sustaining change that have already been referred to. The first is the struggle many teachers have in coming to terms with the technical and psychological aspects of the change process.

This constitutes what Fullan has called the implementation dip', and explains the levels of resistance characteristically associated with school improvement efforts that focus on classroom change. It is these aspects of the implementation process that are not taken account of in most policy formulations.

The second issue relates to the quality of implementation. Although all policies and programmes will require some adaptation to local context, this is not a licence to dilute an innovation beyond recognition. It is the quality and consistency of implementation that eventually ensures positive impact on student achievement.

Third, most effective school improvement strategies require some form of intervention or active implementation. Whether this is internally or externally initiated, it implies some break with existing practice, with all that entails. Policy therefore has to be concerned with helping teachers through the change process, as well as the quality of implementation itself.

Most governments now identify targets for achievement in key learning areas. If these targets are to be realised central policies need to incorporate three further elements. The first is making available to schools and local agencies strategies to assist them in realising the goals they have identified, remembering of course that all schools are at different levels of effectiveness. Instead of every school 're-inventing the wheel' Governments should be encouraging the development and piloting of curriculum and instructional programmes that directly address in implementable ways the targets that they and schools are setting.

Second, if this could be achieved - a range of policy options related to programmes that really work - then schools could begin to select from among a range of options those strategies that address the particular targets they have set, and the learning needs of their students. With a such series of program options available, schools are then in a position to address more directly the crucial issues of staff development, capacity building and consistency of implementation that are so necessary for ensuring student achievement. The school-level context can facilitate, and to a great extent, determine, successful policy implementation.

Third, Governments and NGOs would then be in a position to target funding to those schools in the greatest need in the far more secure knowledge that what they were going to do would achieve the goals the system as a whole had set itself. In order to challenge schools to be the best they can be, and to support program development and capacity building, a local infrastructure also needs to be developed.

Educational Reforms for Effective Learning

Schools are created for the express purpose of providing a certain type of educational experience, which is called the curriculum. The curriculum represents what school policy-makers in a community believe young people need to know in order to develop into good and productive adults. In effect, the curriculum represents a social bet. It is what the older generation thinks the young will need in order to live well in the 21st century.

Curriculum decisions are very important. If the curriculum turns out to be a losing bet, the social consequences are severe. In his voluminous study, A Place Called School, John Goodlad examined a wide range of documents that have tried to define the purposes of American schooling in the past 300 years. He found four broad goals:

1. Academic, including a broad array of knowledge and intellectual skills
2. Vocational, aimed at readiness for the world of work and economic responsibilities
3. Social and civic, including skills and behavior for participating in a complex democratic society

4. Personal, including the development of individual talent and self-expression.

Goodlad included these four areas in questionnaires distributed to parents, students, and teachers. Teachers rated all four "very important" while the other groups indicated preferences. When pushed to select one as having top priority, half the teachers and parents chose the intellectual area. Students spread their preferences fairly even among all four categories. When it comes to selecting the purpose of schools, both those who are its clients and those who provide its services resist interpreting the role of school narrowly.

As technological change overtakes rural and urban communities everywhere in America, do tribal communities guide or participate in a modification or revision of curricula that accurately reflects the unique academic, vocational, social, and personal needs of their children? The last decades of the 20th Century were not kind to Indian children who now make up the poorest segment of society. Contemporary social problems threaten to children and their schools. An increasing number of Indian children live under conditions characterized by extreme stress, chronic poverty, crime, and lack of adult guidance. Their well-being is threatened by violence, substance abuse, AIDS, child abuse, suicide, and homelessness. Frustrated and feeling powerless, many youths escape into the trappings of the material American world-loud music, video games, cults, movies, television, or cruising shopping malls.

These activities place many young Indians at risk of dropping out of school. Students at risk of dropping out tend to get lower grades, perform below grade level academically, are older than the average student at their grade level because of previous retention, and have serious behavior problems in school. Latham reports that "[A] disproportionately large number of minority students are inappropriately classified as learning disabled (LD)." Ysseldyke, Algozzine, and Richey reported that "the number of minority and low socio-economic status children thought to evidence academic difficulty and behavior problems was at least twice as high ... as for other students"

The impact of television has dramatically modified the values system of communities, so much so that Cable TV seems to be finishing the work of Custer. Cable and satellite technology have enabled television and public media imagery to affect even the values of rural, isolated communities. It has been blamed for an array of crises and behavior problems, from a lack of discipline and concentration to passivity, from decline in scholastic achievement to family tensions and especially violence. General entertainment programs and even television commercials have been criticized for promoting violence, stereotyping, and unfair and unhealthy consumer practices.

A 1992 study by the American Psychological Association concluded that unregulated viewing not only robs children of both play and study time, but also leads to increases in prejudice, health problems, and aggressive behavior. Most books on Indian education begin in the years 1492 or 1607. To accept that, one would need to assume that there was a vacuum in Indian education prior to Contact. Traditional methodology was "brain-based," and involved modeling and oral, experiential, and cooperative learning. The classroom was the hands-on environment. The facilitator was the community of elders, parents, and peers.

Learning was life-long, from cradleboard to grave. The next few centuries were marked by colonial government, church, and federal policy experiments. These ventures were rationalized as efforts to "civilize" those who were perceived as "heathens." The indigenous people were viewed as obstacles to the opening of lands for raw materials to fuel a burgeoning American economy. Historically, Indian education was the "battering ram" with Indian children as the door that opened tribal communities to Euro-American exploitation. School curricula, based on religious beliefs and/or trade skills, were the means for assimilating young Indians into the dominant society.

This suppression of Indian identity extended beyond the schools with federal prohibitions against spiritual and cultural rites/rights. This adversarial relationship continued for more than two centuries. The practice of repressing Indian identity triggered the construction of twenty-five off-reservation boarding schools in the 1890s to remove Indian children from their homes and communities. The Meriam Report in 1928 criticized this practice as being "at variance with modern views of education and social work". It also exposed the acute poverty on reservations.

In 1933, Commissioner of Indian Affairs John Collier moved to end allotment of Indian lands, to implement recommendations of the Meriam Report and to localize BIA schools. In 1934, Congress passed legislation, which transferred the responsibility for education of Indian children to nearby public schools.

Beginning in the Sixties with the War on Poverty, another wave of progressive reform occurred. The importance of pre-K was finally recognized and

Headstart programs were initiated to make up for early learning deficit and language delay. Federally legislated reform initiatives influenced the restructuring of classrooms in both urban and rural communities. The Indian Education Act of 1972 amended several major U.S. Office of Education programs, including Title I, and placed some educational governance in the hands of native parents and communities. The Indian Self-Determination and Education Assistance Act of 1975 responded to a growing demand from tribal communities for authority and control by tribal communities of educational institutions.

Although the 1980s appeared to be an era stymied by a lack of nationwide educational vision and a shortage of stable leadership in federal Indian education programs (OIEP and OIE). The National Indian Education Association and American Indian Higher Education Consortium promoted enriched instruction and curriculum for native students as a moral and legal imperative. National reform efforts brought increasing demands from teachers for professional respect and salary levels; charges from the public for greater accountability from schools; rapid technological advances; and an economy interdependent with the rest of the world and hungry for well-educated, thoughtful workers.

The current wave of American school reform can be traced to the study, *A Nation at Risk*, and to the publication of other reports with similar conclusions which stimulated a nationwide drive to improve public school education in the 1980s. As part of this nationwide effort, the U.S. Department of Education Indian Nations at Risk Task Force, in its published report in 1991, Indian Nations at Risk, again uncovered frightening evidence of education deficit and propelled renewed interest in improved educational achievement levels among communities of tribal people.

In 1994, the newly adopted Title I of the Improving America's School Act (IASA) recommended the use of its funds for schoolwide improvement efforts in schools with high concentrations of disadvantaged children. The Eisenhower Professional Development Program emphasized schoolwide reform and gave school staff the flexibility to design and implement school improvement strategies. Effective Schooling is a process by which all students, from early childhood through life, learn an intended curriculum in adherence to a stated mission, goals, and plan of operation. The underlying assumptions are:

— That all students can and will learn,

— That schools can make a difference,

— That what schools care about is then what they will teach and what students will learn,and

— That evidence of school improvement is based on student outcomes.

Effective Schools Movement

By 1994, the federal government had primary responsibility to provide basic support for two types of schools: tribal grant or Bureau of Indian Affairs (BIA) operated schools and state school districts that have Indian students living on trust-status land within the district. Self-determination legislation authorized the BIA to contract with tribes so the tribes could start new schools and/or to take over the operation of BIA schools.

The K-12 basic instructional programs in the 93 BIAoperated and 92 BIA-contract [now grant] schools served only 45,186 students.

Bureau schools had become, in effect, a system specializing in and containing high percentages of children with unusual circumstances and particular needs. Many of the children were "at risk" and/or came from geographically isolated areas. For some, BIA-funded education was their only option. In introducing the Effective Schools Movement to BIA and grant schools, the OIEP invited principals, line officers, and tribal college personnel to develop an appropriate model and action plan based on the Effective Schools correlates.

The OIEP then identified professional monitoring teams composed of a variety of stakeholders in Indian schools. Utilizing extensive instrumentation, the teams conducted thorough 3-4 day on-site examinations gathering information from existing program data, through classroom observation, and by interviewing administrators, faculty, students, and parents. This included information gathered on each school's practices regarding written curricula, instructional methodology and pedagogy, parental involvement, on-site staff development, and cultural relevance.

In 1989, an education advisory group, representing a wide range of practitioners and other stakeholders,was expanded to create the Bureau Effective Schools Team (BEST). The team worked to actively promote high student, staff, and school expectations for success, and to plan, monitor, evaluate, and assist self-selected schools as they progressed through the long-range Effective Schools improvement process. Scholarship grants enabled local school effectiveness teams to participate in regional School Effectiveness Team training programs.

Policy Reform Strategies

Bold policy reforms are needed in order to accelerate education development. The policy reforms need to be sustained over time and, given the magnitude of the challenges and the economical constraints of developing countries, implemented in partnerships of national governments, civil society and donors. As education policy priorities in developing countries have to compete for the limited sources available, such policy reforms require the development of investment programs with the same characteristics, namely sustained over time and implemented in partnerships, strategically sharing the responsibility for the financing and provision of schooling among governments, private providers, parents and non-governmental organisations (NGOs).

The required bold policy reforms that Verspoor argues for should consist of strategies that are aimed at quality improvement, committed to increasing equity, and emphasise institutional strengthening and capacity building. Quality education is needed to contribute to the successful acquisition of 21 century educational goals such as students' ability to apply knowledge, think independently, collaborate with others, and develop lifelong learning skills. Moreover, quality education systems have high participation rates and efficient student flows, and are expected to provide the highest returns on investment because they result in higher learning achievement and partly pay for themselves through efficiency gains.

The pursuit of quality demands a multi-faceted reform strategy that addresses the improvement of basic conditions for learning, of curricula and assessment approaches, and of teacher development in a coherent and comprehensive way. Within this context a few aspects must be emphasised, namely the importance of early childhood education, the use of new technologies in education, and the monitoring of educational progress and outcomes.

Comprehensive and coherent policy interventions All too often reforms fail because of lack of alignment between policy interventions. This underlines the importance of developing comprehensive programs that address the improvement of teaching and learning in a consistent way. These programs should focus on the improvement of basic conditions for learning, curricula and assessment practices, and the quality of the teaching force. Following issues as important for effective education:

— the regular functioning of schools taking into account local 'calendars';

— school health and meals programs;

— enrolment at the usual school age;

— sufficient textbooks and other materials;

— reasonable student-teacher ratios;

— well-equipped classrooms and schools, including facilities as sanitation and clean water (especially important for girls).

The improvement of curricula and assessment practices should be geared towards enhancing their relevance to the context of schooling and students' preparation for the world of work and further learning. An overload of curriculum content should be avoided, and the emphasis in both curricula and assessment procedures should be on strategies that promote understanding, application, and problem solving skills. In addition to core knowledge skills in literacy, numeracy and civic education, curricula of the different sectors should address the countries' challenges by incorporating health issues such as reproductive health and HIV/AIDS transmission and prevention.

Moreover, students should be prepared for the world of work and provided with lifelong learning skills by developing their problem-solving skills, their ability to acquire and synthesise information, and their ability to learn. With regard to the implementation of these curricula it will be important that those pedagogical approaches are chosen that address the diversity of linguistic experiences and learning abilities of the students and that carefully monitor learners' progress and allow for differences in learning pace.

All this will require high-quality curriculum materials that fit the specific context of the school setting as well as well-trained and motivated teachers. To improve the quality of the teaching force, teacher education (including in-service education) should reform radically so that it becomes a process of lifelong learning in which teachers acquire the skills and motivation to apply the new curriculum orientations mentioned above. Several promising options are available for providing such support, including the use of ICT-based approaches, school-based programs, teacher resource centres and teacher networks.

It will be worthwhile to explore the potentials of these approaches, also in terms of providing affordable support to large numbers of teachers. Furthermore, teachers' work conditions (administrative, management, support, materials) should be improved such that teachers can carry out their work as expected. Teacher salaries must be such that they allow teachers to commit themselves full-time to teaching. Professional recognition and support will help motivate teachers once these more attractive employment conditions are in place. As Avalos argues policies should be aimed at building a constructive social image of the teaching profession.

The quality of early childhood development programs—especially the comprehensive ones that include cognitive, health and nutrition interventions - correlates overwhelmingly with primary school enrolment rates, enrolment age, academic performance and dropout and repetition rates. Because of these effects on student readiness low-cost early childhood development programs deserve much support as part of education sector reform. Programs that take local culture and practices into account are more likely to be sustainable, affordable and accessible.

New information and communication technologies (ICTs) provide powerful new opportunities for advancing human development and improving the quality of education. The potentials of the technology revolution will only be realised, however, if there is national capacity to explore opportunities, to adapt technology to the country's needs, and to manage the risks of technological change.

Concerns in many countries include the lack of an economic environment that encourages innovation, of limited resources and high telecommunications and Internet costs, and the lack of a clear policy and vision on the use of technology in education. As cost is still a barrier to widespread application in the poorest countries, many countries have to reform their telecommunications and power sector before they can take education applications of new technologies to scale.

As actual learning achievement is the real measure for success, effective education reform needs reliable data on inputs and outcomes of education investments and on classroom processes. In other words, it is necessary to have a good and reliable monitoring system in place that gathers information on inputs and outcomes at different levels in the education system.

In many developing countries such a system is lacking and this type of information is not regularly collected and analysed. Given this concern, Berryman, amongst others, recommends that education systems build a diagnostic and analytical capacity that will allow learning about how to improve student achievement. Furthermore, the system's actors should be held accountable for student learning.

In Berryman's view "accountability for learning is typically assigned to the student, not to the system. ... Accountability for the adults in the systems seems to mean solely conformity to rules, edicts and regulations. To promote quality improvement, policymakers will need to shift accountability from rules to student learning." Noteworthy in this context is to mention the Southern African Consortium for the Measurement of Educational Quality (SACMEQ), an initiative of a number of African countries (and supported by the International Institute for Educational Planning (IIEP) of UNESCO) to improve national education statistics and monitor student learning through standardised tests to a sample of learners.

Besides quality improvement, a commitment to equity is also important in order to achieve 'education for all'. Several challenges have to be addressed in this respect. A first key priority is to increase the initial enrolment of girls, especially in rural areas. This problem is serious as about 60% of the out-of-school children are girls. Urban-rural disparities also have to be dealt with; e.g. in the capital cities of Ethiopia and Mali 80% or more children enrol in primary education compared with 20% or less in the rural areas.

Equity is also determined by the quality of education that children receive and by the disparity in performance. Schools in rural areas often have additional obstacles to providing quality education, such as teacher absenteeism, lower educational attainment, less availability of instructional materials, and poorly built classrooms. Parents in rural areas are often asked to contribute to the cost of schooling more than parents in urban areas.

At least one million additional teachers are needed in Africa in order to reach a situation of universal education. African countries will need to build more than 150.000 new classrooms per year over the next 15 years, many of them in rural areas. Considering these challenges, new models for providing education have to be sought in order to reach out to excluded groups such as the poor, rural populations and girls and work towards education for all. These models should emphasise:

— quality schooling appropriate for rural conditions;

— education strategies that address the demand- and supply-side obstacles facing hard-to-reach groups;

— community involvement in school operations and the management of classrooms;

— teacher training and decentralised provision of on-the-job teacher support and a

— restructuring of the teaching profession; decentralisation planning and resource management responsibilities to communities and district education offices.

Strategies to reach universal high-quality education have led to a move away from traditional, highly centralised management models towards models of decentralised planning and putting management responsibilities with communities and district offices. This requires capacity building at all levels of the system. Higher education institutions, especially universities, have a critical role to play in this respect as they are the places where national capacity and leadership in education is trained and where research and development capabilities are developed and kept on the high level needed for the dynamic processes of improvement and reform.

To unleash the potential of higher education's contribution to society, the resources committed to higher education should be increased and the efficiency with which resources are used should be improved. According to Verspoor, universities and other higher education institutions have to be made responsible for managing their resources and defining institutional policy. Moreover, a radical rethinking of approaches to broadening university access will have to take place in many countries.

The emergence of a global knowledge-based economy, and the need for lifelong learning opportunities for workers to upgrade their skills and maintain their competitiveness, are creating new pressures to raise university enrolments. With the severe resource and management constraints, however, the capacity of universities cannot easily be expanded. Therefore new approaches and institutional arrangements are needed that help to overcome the costs, access and quality problems in higher education.

At the local and regional level priority should be given to strengthening the capacity for allocating resources, managing teaching staff, and planning and implementing investment programs. The focus hereby should be on school management committees, parent-teacher associations, and structures for community participation (e.g. village education committees). While capacity building is at the core of many reform program nowadays, there is still a lot to be learned.

Samoff notes that the rhetoric of capacity building has been accompanied by stagnating or declining capacity, especially in the domain of education. He urges that more research is needed to understand why shortages exist even in areas where there have been decades of training programs. Moreover, reform policies and implementation strategies will have to be designed to learn from experiences and to support programs long enough to allow them to build capacity.

Implementing Reform Strategies

Many researchers and educators have studied educational reform strategies in developing countries and how these are related to the capacity for change at the school level. A first important consideration in formulating reform strategies should be the financial sustainability. Verspoor argues that education policy reforms require the development of investment programs sustained over time and implemented in partnerships in which the responsibility for the financing and provision of schooling is shared among governments, private providers and non-governmental organisations (NGOs). Even when such partnerships are in place, education improvement programs will usually have considerable implications for government budgets.

New financing policies and management are needed that define clear priorities for public resource allocation, increase the effectiveness of public spending, include strategies for diversifying funding sources beyond the public sector ('partnership of all stakeholders'; increased role of private-for-profit and non-for-profit providers, under the condition of delivering quality education), and allocate additional public resources to the sector.

The development of a self-sufficient and sustainable formal system over time in cooperation with donors and NGOs will swing the balance back to the government being responsible for improving and maintaining the quality of its own system. This will require both 'care' and 'courage' on both sides. 'Care' from the donors and NGOs to assist the government to develop its capacity to do this and 'courage' on the part of the government to take increasing responsibility for solving its own problems and becoming more independent".

Many reform policies are based on the implicit assumption that policy implementation is an event rather than a process. However, that the way districts, local agencies, schools and teachers put reforms into practice should be seen as a process of change which often takes many years. Because of its process character, a requirement for change to succeed and have impact is a certain amount of 'environmental stability', both in terms of political and financial support.

As institutions and individuals may differ in their resource and management conditions, policymakers should utilise this variation in innovation capability in their reform strategies. Strategies should be developed that allow certain 'forerunner' institutes or schools to build up experience with the reform and develop these into examples of 'best practice', while the same period is used to strengthen the innovation capability of the 'follower' schools through focused support programs. This implies that policymakers should aim for regional or even local (school) specific changes rather than system-wide changes.

5

Conflict between Technology and Participation

Education reforms share one political predicament that distinguishes them from other types of reform. They must maximize technocratic expertise and civic participation simultaneously. The requirement that education reforms meet high technocratic standards is predicated on the recognition that most education systems are complex and massive, usually comprising the largest component of the federal budget.

Reformers need to be able to digest complex diagnoses of the problems, sort out the factors that hinder and foster learning, be cognizant of different pedagogical methodologies, understand demographics of diverse school districts and inter-government finance, and devise costeffective solutions that maximize performance incentives.

The requirement that education reforms meet high participation standards is predicated on two principles: a democratic ideal and a pragmatic consideration. The democratic ideal is that, given that education reforms touch many citizens and interest groups in the country, it is incumbent upon democratic nations to incorporate the views of as many actors as possible. The pragmatic consideration is the notion, common among international donors, that education reforms stand a higher chance of implementation if affected groups come to "own" the reforms. This sense of ownership emerges if societal actors are made to participate in policy formulation.

The problem is that these dual requirements are, often, in conflict with each other. The requirement that reforms meet high technocratic standards leads to political practices that jeopardize participation: reducing the number of actors to only those who are technically qualified, generating coherence (rather than pluralism) within the change team, discussing only the technical merits of policy, granting disproportionate powers to technical experts.

Technocratism infuses reforms with specialized knowledge at the expense of inclusiveness. Likewise, the requirement that reforms meet inclusionary standards introduces political practices that jeopardize technical purity: inviting many actors to the design board, not just experts; considering the impact of reforms on different groups, not simply examining the technical merits of reform; striving for consensus among disparate groups, not just among like-minded technical experts; proposing solutions that are culturally palatable, not just what is technically optimal.

Participationism infuses reforms with pluralism at the expense of technical purity. Education reforms are politically complex because they require combining these two conflicting objectives. Education reformers are continuously torn by the need to be technocratically sound and inclusionary, at times losing patience with the latter goal.

Societal actors in turn often have no stomach for the hard choices that technical experts seek to solve. Rather than dismiss the existence of this tradeoff, it is important instead to theorize about its exact parameters. In most Latin American countries in the 1991-2000 decade: the average turnover rate was 2.81 years, up from 2.45 in the 1969-1990 period. Argentina, Brazil, Chile, the Dominican Republic, El Salvador, Honduras, Nicaragua and Panama registered the highest increases in tenure stability in comparison to their own past. Tenure in office also increased, although to a lesser extent, in Bolivia, Costa Rica, Peru, Venezuela, and Uruguay. Stability declined in Mexico, but its turnover rates still remain high.

Furthermore, stability increased even in countries that experienced transitions from authoritarianism to democracy in the 1990s. In Chile and Panama, for instance, turnover rates improved in the democratic 1990s relative to the authoritarian 1980s. In Mexico, turnover rates stayed the same despite the breakdown of stable authoritarianism. In Nicaragua and Paraguay, however, turnover rates declined significantly with the transition to democracy. Surprisingly, turnover rates of education ministers compares favorably with turnover rates of finance ministers in the 1990s, although the record is uneven.

Some countries with presumed improvements in the power of ministries did not generate impressive reform accomplishments in the 1990s. And countries in which the power of the education ministry declined have achieved serious reforms. Theoretically, the reason that long tenure, or high technocracy in general, is not a sufficient cause of reforms is that there are other intervening variables between the supply side of reforms and implementation. Bolstering the supply side of reform is not sufficient for consolidating change.

Furthermore, bolstering the supply side of reform can generate new sets of problems, the most important of which is probably alienating civil society, or delinking the state and civil society. In the politics of education reform, researchers have focused on a number of intermediate institutional and coalitional variables: union strength and unity, coalitions among and within in-groups and out-groups, partnerships with international financial institutions, constitutional obstacles and types of alliances between national and sub-national actors. A less explored but equally crucial intermediate variable is features of the party system.

Willis et al. argue that key issue is "where party leaders preside". If parties control nominations for congress and governors, then the leverage of subnational actors will diminish-parties will more often than not slight the preferences of subnational actors. Another predictive criteria is levels of inter-party conflict. Essentially, the lower the degree of political party conflict, the less likely that societal and interest group discontent will flourish. Affected interest groups that lack institutional avenues to channel their discontent will become less willing to engage in activism. Unions in particular are affected by this.

While the nature of state-union conflict is shaped by many factors, including levels of external and internal competition, they can also be susceptible to party variables. According to Norden, party systems can vary in the extent to which they are cooperative or conflictive. Norden, like many other scholars, focuses on levels of conflict among the parties. Yet, it is also important to take into consideration conflicts between the ruling party and the Executive. Taking into consideration both inter-party conflicts and executive ruling party conflicts, one can establish the following categories of party conflict, ranging from very low to very high levels. Very-low levels of party conflict. Zero levels of party conflict is inconceivable in democracies, by definition.

The politics of education reform can thus vary according to two dimensions: types of reform (i.e., levels of policy boldness) and institutional context (e.g., levels of party conflict). Essentially, the higher the policy boldness and the higher the level of party conflict, the higher the level of societal unrest, and hence lower the chances of implementation.

The reform experience of Argentina in the past two decades provides evidence for these hypotheses. Different models of decision making were attempted, resulting in a wide array of policy proposals, of varying degree of boldness, occurring both at the national and provincial levels. These proposals generated different degrees of statesociety conflict with different levels of implementation. Levels of inter-party level conflict help explain these different implementation outcomes.

Although nominally a democracy with a two-party system, the province of San Luis had a semi autocratic political system. The governor had been elected continuously since 1983 with ample margins, the ruling party was relatively obsequious, and civil society and opposition parties were fairly acquiescent. The result was high implementation, with low levels of conflict.

Participation in Lifelong Learning

Lifelong Learning has a major contribution to make towards providing those who are in employment and those looking for work with upto-date skills and knowledge. As a result, new demands have been placed on colleges of further education to increase provision and to widen access to education and training. This will require greater flexibility in recruitment and new approaches to teaching and learning including the development and use of ICT. To contribute towards the achievement of the objectives of Lifelong Learning, colleges of further education are required to expand significantly and improve learning opportunities for all sections of the community.

The objectives of the Lifelong Learning strategy have implications for the development of ICT. They are to:

— increase significantly adult participation in vocational education and training, including access to further and higher education and training from groups previously under-represented;

— emphasise the development of basic and key skills;

— ensure greater ease of progression through the system of qualifications;

— provide a more coherent relationship between education and training provision and the skills needed for the regional economy;

— enhance collaboration between education and training providers and the world of business and industry;

— enhance significantly the information and communication skills of teachers, instructors and students;

— sustain and improve the quality of provision and enhance the performance across the education and training sectors.

In Northern Ireland, the government has drawn up an action plan for the next three years to ensure the objectives of the Lifelong Learning strategy are achieved and a new culture of lifelong learning is established. A number of targets set by the action plan have major implications for the further education sector. These include:

— launching the UfI in 2000 to promote and market education and training;
— developing more flexible modes of provision so as to facilitate increased participation in learning;
— introducing a Strategic Collaboration Fund in 1999 to enhance partnership in adult education;
— education and training between further education colleges and the main stakeholders;
— expanding significantly participation in further education by 8,000 full-time and part-time places by 2002.

Central to the success of the strategy for Lifelong Learning is the UfI which will build on the NGfL. These initiatives will exploit modern information and communication technologies, including the Internet and CD-ROMs, to make learning more flexible, available and cost-effective. By the year 2000, the UfI will be launched nationally and will develop close links with private organisations, colleges of further education and schools. The targets for the NGfL by 2002 include connecting all schools, colleges, universities and public libraries to the NGfL, and ensuring that serving lecturers feel confident and are competent to teach using ICT within the curriculum.

A Northern Ireland Network for Education (NINE) has been established as the local node for NGfL and the further education sector has a major role to play in its development. The development and use of ICT in teaching and learning varies considerably between programme areas. In computer studies, construction and engineering, ICT is used regularly and effectively by about half of lecturers. Approximately one-quarter of lecturers in business, science, and in programmes for students with special learning difficulties and disabilities have developed a good level of competence in ICT and have the confidence to plan and use it in their teaching strategies.

Less than one-tenth of lecturers in art and design, health and social care, leisure and tourism and basic skills programmes plan their work to provide students with the opportunity to learn through ICT related tasks. In all colleges, there are enthusiastic staff committed to using ICT to enhance students' learning. They are aware of the many initiatives to develop educational technology and have made a good start to use existing ICT resources to plan and support teaching in a range of programme areas.

Most staff are not aware, however, of the potential of ICT to support and improve teaching and learning. They lack confidence in using new technology and have not been provided with suitable opportunities to develop competence in ICT and to integrate it into their teaching methods. In some programme areas, committed staff are not able to use ICT effectively because of insufficient or outdated computer systems and ICT infrastructures or a limited range of software. They are also hindered by the lack of, or inadequate implementation of strategies for ICT development.

Approximately half the colleges are implementing suitable policies and strategies for the development of ICT and are benefiting from their investments. Staff are starting to integrate ICT successfully into teaching and learning methods and the colleges are investigating new approaches to use ICT to increase participation rates in education. Only a small number of colleges assess the ICT skills of all new students to identify the level of support required to help them use the ICT resources effectively. In the other colleges, the initial assessment of students' ICT skills is left to the discretion of individual programme co-ordinators.

All colleges enrol students with a wide range of competences in ICT. Many have excellent skills in ICT, however, a significant number progress from school to full-time and part-time courses with poor ICT skills and are unable to cope sufficiently with the demands of their courses. For example, in a fulltime technician course in construction, approximately half of the students had no previous experience of ICT and could not engage in a simple computer-assisted-drafting exercise. The lecturer was given no information about the students' level of competence in ICT and was unable to provide appropriate support during the lesson.

Almost all colleges provide full-time students on vocational courses with an induction programme of basic ICT skills consisting of either timetabled classes or support in open learning centres. The quality of this support is usually good. Students acquire basic competences and are able to word-process, create spreadsheets and interrogate databases although few are accredited with a qualification. Most full-time students on academic courses are not provided with planned opportunities to learn relevant ICT skills. Students enrolled on part-time vocational courses are seldom provided with induction programmes and they develop their ICT skills only when it is needed as part of their course. The provision for part-time students wishing to address significant weaknesses in ICT is generally inadequate.

Only a minority are provided with good guidance on relevant courses and open access facilities to achieve accreditation in basic ICT skills. In most colleges, students with learning difficulties and/or disabilities have good access to ICT facilities. They are provided with up to three hours each week to develop a wide range of experiences in ICT including word-processing, CD-ROMs, Internet and the use of electronic mail (E-mail). Approximately half the colleges are using ICT to improve access to further education and widen participation.

One effective strategy is to transport high specification laptop computer systems to community and outreach centres to deliver a range of part-time courses in IT. This provision has increased significantly the participation of adult community groups in further education. Most of the adults enrolled on the courses have had little or no previous experience of further education and lack confidence in their ability to learn. The courses are well planned and prepared and provide the students with challenging learning experiences. The students are encouraged to learn independently and are motivated to achieve qualifications in IT.

Another innovative strategy for widening participation is the Adapt project where a college is piloting a new computer-based learning system. This allows students from a distant location using high specification, on-line computer facilities to connect to a central CD-ROM server based in the college and provides access to a wide range of training programmes customised to meet individual requirements. Small to medium enterprises in agriculture, retail and tourism involving 120 managers ranging in age from 30 to 70 have been selected for the pilot.

Most of these students have not participated previously in further education and have little experience of ICT. The aim of the project is to accelerate the acquisition of new ICT skills and to increase the competitiveness of industry. The above strategies indicate that widening participation to further education is best achieved by increasing the flexibility of the ICT facilities available to students and providing them with good access to relevant information and well designed learning materials.

In about half the colleges open access centres with up-to-date computer systems are well organised and utilised by students from all vocational areas. They are encouraging students to take greater responsibility for their own learning and to work independently. A further one-quarter of colleges have made a good start towards using the open access centres to achieve their full potential to support the students' learning. In the remaining colleges, the centres are poorly organised and not well utilised by students. Staff in these centres are not clear on their roles and responsibilities and do not provide students with suitable guidance and support.

In addition, there is limited good quality software and other resources. As a result, students are not motivated and do not utilise fully the computer systems. The main use by students of the computer systems in open access centres is limited to word-processing assignments and creating spreadsheets. The use of databases is confined mainly to technology-based and business-related curriculum areas. Students benefit most from open access centres when they engage in challenging computer-based tasks set by their vocational tutors and have developed the necessary ICT skills to make full use of the computer systems.

Although all colleges are connected to the Internet, most have few connection points and provide limited access for students. In addition, few staff have incorporated the application of the Internet into their teaching methods. As a result, the Internet is not well used to support students' learning. A minority of students use it to obtain information or data on specialist areas for their assignment work. Most, however, do not have sufficient skills to use it competently and spend too much time collecting unnecessary information. In colleges with open access arrangements to the Internet, staff are encouraged to integrate its use into their teaching methods and to provide the students with suitable support in developing their expertise to use it effectively.

Students on higher education courses in four colleges benefit significantly from using the Joint Academic Network (JANET) to communicate with local universities and use a range of information sources including video conferencing. In all colleges, there is wide use of video recordings in vocational and most academic courses. In the best practice, the use of video recordings is planned and integrated effectively into the students' learning. Students benefit from observing welldocumented relevant experiences recorded on video and use them to discuss and apply them to their work. Frequently, however, the video is watched out of context by students who are unable to understand its relevance to their subject area.

Many video recordings used in teaching are outdated. Audio tapes are used effectively in all colleges, mainly in courses in modern languages and media studies. In a few colleges, high quality specialist computer-based audio facilities are used to teach music courses. They provide students with excellent experiences in working with electronic-based music. The majority of lecturers in academic studies have not acquired a basic level of competence in the use of ICT. In English, geography, history and mathematics, there are almost no computer-based learning materials available for students, even in colleges with well organised open access centres and good ICT facilities.

Two colleges provide a limited range of CD-ROMs and software application packages in mathematics for students to learn independently. A small number of students use ICT to present their work using word-processing, particularly in English. Exceptionally, one or two students use the Internet to retrieve information for use in their assignments. They obtain authentic material on a wide range of specific topics which considerably broadens their vocabulary. In most colleges, good use is made of video and audio equipment on GCSE and GCE A level courses in modern languages for students to present, practise and consolidate their language skills.

Satellite television and video conferencing are used by students in two colleges to communicate with language students in other countries. These students have excellent learning experiences and gain a good understanding of the cultures associated with the language development. One college has commissioned a new computer-based language laboratory which has the facility to link to the Internet. Students have good opportunities to work independently and co-operate well with other students in group projects. The use of the laboratory is not yet exploited to its full potential. There is a considerable variation in the competence of lecturers of modern languages to integrate ICT into their teaching strategies. In two colleges, all lecturers have had effective staff development on the use of the Internet and confidently create appropriate websites. The majority of lecturers do not, however, use ICT sufficiently to enhance the students' learning.

The planned use of ICT in teaching and learning is limited in art and design to those lecturers with specific interest in ICT and, there is significant variation in the degree to which the staff are able to use ICT in teaching and learning. The level of competence of many lecturers is limited to the use of word-processing, databases and spreadsheets and the majority have not progressed to using the broader applications of ICT, for example, CD-ROMs in a formal teaching situation. In contrast, considerable use is made of CD-ROMs by art and design students, for example, in the research of progression opportunities in employment and higher education and in the research of historical and contemporary art and design.

Many students use ICT to produce graphics but it is rarely used for three-dimensional, textiles and fashion or interior and spacial design. Many colleges have retained a small number of Apple Macintosh machines solely for art and design purposes but they are usually out of date and poorly maintained. The quality and quantity of hardware installed with specialist art and design software is, in the majority of cases, poor. In a few instances there are small numbers of up-to-date machines with appropriate software; these are heavily used and, as a result, are frequently out of order.

While the use of digital cameras has been introduced successfully in a small number of colleges there are large numbers of students wishing to access a single camera. The use and development of ICT in teaching and learning in art and design are underdeveloped and the quality and standards of specialist software and hardware are inadequate. The use of ICT in basic skills is largely limited to old and slow machines running dated and limited software packages.

Lecturers, however, do manage to maximise the potential of these facilities and many students succeed in developing a basic range of keyboarding skills in word-processing and drafting letters. In one college the students on basic skills programmes use very simple software packages to develop their number skills and improve their understanding of measurement, height, weight and time. Problems with hardware and its incompatibility with main college ICT facilities cause problems in many colleges which often result in students being unfamiliar with the different operating systems and unable to use the ICT facilities in the main college library or open learning centre.

In only one college are interactive learning programmes in basic skills used to good effect. The IT skills of the majority of students are poor. The work is highly prescriptive and most of the students require regular direction and intervention from their tutors. In many cases the students are not proficient at accessing software, files and databases or in saving and printing their own work. The level of investment in ICT for basic skill classes is poor. In many colleges the classes are located in cramped and damp mobiles and are allocated the oldest computers and printers, some of which are almost obsolete.

In one college the recent purchase of new computers has not been matched with the supply of appropriate software, however, funds have been allocated to rectify this in the coming year. In around half of the colleges the move towards mainly personal computer (PC) hardware has disadvantaged many of the students in basic skills who are still taught mainly on older systems. In basic skills the use of ICT is not well developed and students are disadvantaged by the allocation of old machines no longer required by other departments and courses.

All colleges need to invest in the specialist hardware and software for basic skills work and in doing so to ensure that the operating systems are compatible with the college's open access ICT facilities. In the majority of classes where ICT is used by vocational lecturers, the quality of teaching and learning is good. In one college, for example, a lecturer has trained students to use the Internet to research the social and economic profiles of countries and to evaluate export marketing opportunities. The key skill classes in IT are well planned and provide students with good opportunities to develop competence across all the elements of the key skill.

In most colleges, the IT lecturers collaborate with the vocational specialists to integrate the teaching of the key skill in an appropriate vocational context. Students have good opportunities, for example, to integrate their knowledge of spreadsheet techniques with cash flow forecasts. The use of ICT, however, in assignment briefs is underdeveloped in the majority of colleges and the students have insufficient opportunities to develop and reinforce the skills learned in the IT classes. Most of the students have satisfactory or better IT skills, especially in word-processing, spreadsheets and databases.

A significant minority of students have poor skills in researching, interpreting and disseminating information from the Internet. In the majority of colleges, the computer rooms are utilised fully for IT key skills classes and most of the computers are stand-alone and dated. In one college, a lecturer who was using an interactive accounting learning package with a Higher National Certificate class did not have access to a networked computer room. A considerable amount of time was wasted installing seven floppy disks on each computer before the class could begin.

Most lecturers in business have developed good skills in IT and a significant minority of them use their own personal computers at home to produce teaching resources. However, most are not confident in the use of ICT in the classroom and their knowledge of the resources which are available is poor. There is insufficient use of ICT in teaching and learning in business and staff require more support in the use of ICT as a teaching tool. In addition, there is insufficient access to networked computer rooms for nearly all business courses.

Students have good opportunities to develop their IT skills when they are integrated effectively into the assignment programme. Although almost all of the lecturers in the vocational area of computing have high levels of expertise in ICT, there is considerable variation in the use of educational technology to improve and enhance the quality of teaching and learning. In most colleges the computing courses are well organised and provide students with good opportunities to develop practical ICT skills in vocationally relevant applications. However, little use is made of computer-based learning techniques.

A small number of lecturers make good use of data projection equipment for software and other demonstrations but most lecturers make insufficient use of presentation software in the delivery of lessons and there are few examples of the use of CD-ROM materials, multimedia packages, video conferencing or the Internet to support learning. In a minority of colleges, the students make good use of the Internet to access technical support sites when designing and developing computer programs. In the majority of colleges, the integration and use of the Internet as a teaching strategy is underdeveloped; student access is often limited and expensive. In about half of the colleges, the resources used to deliver computing do not meet modern standards.

In these colleges many of the computers are unable to run some of the more advanced software tools and the students have insufficient opportunity to use up-to-date computer systems. This inhibits the use of educational technology by lecturers to develop the students' use of relational databases, presentation software and the design of computer programs in programming languages which involve object orientated and event-driven programming. In one-third of colleges, the networks provide students with access to good on-line learning materials where they work independently to develop ICT skills in a variety of industry-standard application packages.

In these colleges, lecturers integrate educational technology effectively into their teaching strategies and the students' learning in computing is enhanced. In computing, while the ICT skills of lecturers are well-developed, there is little integration of ICT into their teaching and learning strategies. The quality of teaching and learning in the use of computer-aided draughting is at different stages of development. In about half of the programmes the work is well developed. The students have very good learning experiences and the quality of their work is excellent. In about one-quarter of the programmes the use of computer-aided draughting is satisfactory and continues to develop.

The students have acquired the basic concepts but still need to develop their expertise in the use of specialist architectural packages. In about one-quarter of the programmes the use of computeraided draughting is at an early stage of development in terms of access to modern hardware, software and developing the skills in a vocational context. However, now that access to the equipment and software is improving these weaknesses should be addressed. Good use is made of ICT in the teaching of environmental science.

Most of the students use spreadsheets for tabulated calculations such as heat loss from buildings and most use word-processors for their assignments. Presentation software is not used extensively. The accommodation and equipment for ICT in about half of the construction programmes are good. The hardware is modern and is located in rooms refurbished with the specialist furnishings. There is modern hardware and software in about onequarter of the programmes but the computers have yet to be linked to an effective network. In construction, the use of ICT is strongest in technician programmes and in the use of software for computer-aided draughting.

The standard of teaching of specialist IT in engineering is never less than satisfactory and is generally good. The majority of the lecturers have worked hard to keep themselves up-to-date with modern engineering technologies and to ensure that students are challenged by well planned lectures, projects and relevant assignments. The quality of the physical resources for use by engineering students has improved dramatically in most colleges during the last three years and, within each college, this normally sets the limit of the match between the experiences which the students receive and the needs of modern industry.

For example, across the colleges, technician students consistently have good or better opportunities to develop their abilities in computeraided design in mechanical and electrical engineering whereas their experiences in modern computer-aided manufacture, the control of mechanical and electrical power systems, and computer-assisted learning in electronics are good or excellent in only around one-half of the colleges. Apart from the development of the specialist IT skills of the students, less than onethird of the lecturers use IT widely as a means to enhance the learning experiences of the students.

In general, the use of the Internet and commercially produced CD-ROMs and computer-assisted learning software is underdeveloped. Two excellent examples were observed where the lecturers had developed their own high quality computerassisted learning software; one lecturer used software effectively to integrate the teaching of engineering science and mathematics to improve the understanding of the students and another lecturer used distance learning material to teach computer-aided design on a course which attracted employees from industry with a wide range of prior experience of computer-aided design.

Technician students demonstrate a satisfactory or good standard of specialist ICT skills, particularly in the computer-aided design of mechanical components and of electronic circuits and systems. In general, they display good standards in the key skill of IT. This contrasts with craft students, the majority of whom do not develop competence in a broad range of IT skills. Few engineering students use the Internet to search out information for themselves. In general, the provision for technician students in engineering to develop their specialist IT skills and their key skills of IT is good and the standards achieved by the students are never less than satisfactory and mostly good or excellent. The provision for craft students is not designed to ensure that all of them have opportunities to develop a wide range of either specialist IT skills or the key skill of IT.

The provision of ICT in health and social care ranges from satisfactory to poor but is mostly poor. In the satisfactory provision, the students have timetabled classes in IT and have access to open learning centres to use computers to word-process assignments, CD-ROMs for information, and the Internet for access to relevant databases such as the Child Care Web Page. In the poor provision, there is little available beyond of the timetabled provision for the key skill of IT. The use of ICT in teaching and learning in health and social care is generally poor; only around 25% is good. The majority of the specialist teachers have little experience in ICT and are unaware of the resources available to support their teaching.

The students have a good understanding of IT because of the key skill of IT and, from their assignments, can undertake competently word-processing, spreadsheets and data presentation. They are less competent in using CD-ROMs and the Internet to access information and databases to support their assignments and projects. The assignment programmes generally have no specific requirements for the students to access CDROMs or the Internet. This is due mainly to the teachers' lack of knowledge of what is available and how its use could be integrated into assignments. The ICT hardware and software resources which are used in health and social care are part of the general college provision.

College libraries and/or open learning centres generally provide information on the CD-ROMs available for the use of students and staff; often, the information provides brief details of what is included on each CDROM. Access to college Internet facilities is expensive for the students. The use of ICT in teaching and learning in health and social care is generally poor. Whilst all specialist teachers have participated in basic ICT training, this has only been developed further in health and social care in a minority of colleges.

The main ICT provision for leisure and tourism students is an average of one taught hour per week in the key skill of IT. In most cases, the vocational lecturers meet with the specialist IT lecturers to identify together appropriate opportunities to develop the key skill through vocational and occupational units of study. ICT is used confidently by less than 10% of leisure and tourism lecturers to improve teaching and learning. In the best examples, the students are required to use the Internet or CD-ROMs to seek and assess information for assignments. The links developed between the vocational tutors and the key skill specialists provide limited opportunities to develop IT skills in vocationally relevant contexts.

Access to ICT facilities in well resourced classrooms and learning resource centres is good in 50% of the colleges. In one college there has been significant investment specifically for leisure and tourism courses. There is a suite of networked multimedia PCs with dedicated technical support. Despite being at an early stage of development, particularly in the purchase of appropriate software for the vocational area, significant steps have been taken to improve the opportunities to integrate ICT into aspects of the leisure and tourism curriculum. The lack of an adequate network infrastructure, however, and generally low level of ICT resources in the remainder of the colleges hinder student access to important sources of ICT based information. The level of ICT knowledge and expertise varies amongst full-time and part-time staff across the vocational area.

In 75% of the colleges the awareness of staff of current ICT developments has been raised through the attendance at staff development courses in the Oxford and Cambridge RSA Computer Literacy and Information Technology (CLAIT) courses and a series of short courses in the use of CD-ROMs, the Internet and Powerpoint. In one college, a specialist IT lecturer has been seconded to assist in the design and delivery of ICT training for all college staff and the lecturers are encouraged to follow a Joint Examining Board certificate in the educational use of IT.

Approximately half of the colleges make good use of ICT as a learning and teaching resource for science. These colleges place a strong emphasis on the use of ICT to develop the science curriculum and tools such as proprietary software, data-logging equipment and the Internet and intranet materials are used well to enhance and enrich the students' learning experiences. In contrast, in the other colleges little use is made of ICT in science classes. In the best practice, the science lecturers give considerable thought and attention to selecting aspects of the curriculum which can be enhanced by the use of ICT.

There is a general shortage of resources for ICT for both staff and students. While many colleges have used funding from the Further Education Programme to enhance and expand software and hardware, generally the staff and students do not have sufficient access to modern equipment and resources. Although many students have access to IT facilities outside normal timetabled classes, they have insufficient access to specialist software. The use of ICT as a teaching and learning resource for science is beginning to be developed in colleges. The quality of the provision varies widely.

Provision for students with learning difficulties and disabilities includes programmes for people with physical disabilities, as well as provision for individuals with mild, moderate or severe learning difficulties. The provision for students with physical disabilities is generally good. Many colleges provide special aids and adaptations which promote inclusive learning for students with physical disabilities. Examples of such aids in use in colleges are the special guard which enables one student with cystic fibrosis to use a computer and the sound facility which provides computer access for blind students.

The provision for students with learning difficulties and disabilities is more variable. In the provision which is good in approximately 20% of the colleges, the students have regular access to computers and good quality software packages. Poor provision is characterised by equipment which is outdated and a lack of staff awareness that ICT can be used to support learning for these students. The use of ICT in teaching and learning for students with learning difficulties and disabilities is generally satisfactory. Students' abilities to use ICT are related directly to the quality of the equipment available, the access which they have to appropriate packages which are relevant and ageappropriate, and the expertise in ICT of the staff supporting these programmes.

Many of the lecturers require additional training if they are to realise the potential of the use of ICT with these students. At times, standards are affected adversely as a consequence of insufficient co-ordination between the specialist lecturers and those who are teaching basic skills. In one college, this is leading to insufficient progression in the development of the students' skills in the use of ICT. The quality of ICT hardware and software resources which is used for students with learning difficulties and disabilities is good in approximately 20% of the colleges.

Staff awareness of the ways in which ICT can be used to support teaching and learning for students with learning difficulties and disabilities is increasing but there remains a need for staff training and development which focuses on the identification and application of specialist equipment for use with these students. In a minority of colleges, the only equipment which is available to the students on a regular basis is outdated. There is a need to upgrade the facilities available for these students and to extend the use of selected software packages to improve the learning of students.

In recent years, all colleges have provided staff development programmes in ICT. To date, about two-thirds of lecturers have acquired a basic level of competence in ICT and a minority have progressed to higher qualifications. In most colleges, a minority of staff from a wide range of vocational areas have benefited from well-organised specialist courses and have achieved high levels of competence in ICT. A few colleges have included technicians in the staff development programmes for ICT training. About half the colleges have carried out an assessment of lecturers' expertise in ICT, usually through a questionnaire. Only one-quarter of colleges have used, however, the results of the assessment to identify clearly areas where there are skills shortages in ICT and to design programmes to meet the specific curricular needs of lecturers.

The staff development programmes provide training mainly in word-processing, spreadsheets, databases, and the use of CD-ROMs and the Internet, but do not focus sufficiently on the use of ICT to support teaching and learning. Few colleges have an effective staff development programme to ensure there are sufficient well-qualified technicians for ICT work. A number of colleges have recruited technicians with high levels of expertise who are able to maintain and commission computer systems, networks, video conferencing equipment and satellite facilities.

They work competently with lecturers and students during lessons to ensure all systems are functional. In the majority of colleges, the technicians have been in long-term employment and have little expertise in the maintenance and commissioning of ICT systems and require significant levels of retraining. Frequently in these colleges, ICT equipment which has failed remains out of service for long periods of time.

Colleges recognise that there is a general shortage of good quality interactive learning materials across all curriculum areas which are suitable for students with a wide range of ability and interests. Approximately one-quarter of colleges have acquired a satisfactory range of commercially-produced interactive learning materials. Lecturers with expertise in ICT have identified and purchased suitable CD-ROMs and specialist software applications which meet specific needs in a range of curriculum areas and promote the use of ICT in teaching and learning.

For example, CD-ROMS are used in health and social care to access relevant information, Autocad software packages are used for students to learn draughting skills, students in travel courses use software for travel accommodation and reservations and accounting software is used for business applications. These packages cater for a wide range of interests and abilities and allow students to work on their own.

The remaining colleges provide students with only a limited range of interactive learning materials which significantly inhibits the effective use of the ICT facilities for teaching and learning. In almost all colleges, there is little use of interactive learning materials to deliver programmes in basic skills. In all colleges, there are only small numbers of lecturers who have benefited from curriculum development initiatives in ICT. Most lecturers do not have sufficient expertise to evaluate or produce relevant and challenging interactive learning materials which allow students to work independently.

The quality of the interactive learning materials is good and has been disseminated to all colleges. In a large college, the lecturers on adult basic education programmes produced a specialist software package for the computer-based assessment of basic skills. Lecturers who have participated in curriculum development initiatives have developed a high-level of awareness of the application of ICT to support teaching and learning. Approximately half the colleges have devised appropriate written policies and strategies for the development and use of ICT across the curriculum.

They are comprehensive and reflect recent Government initiatives aimed at promoting the effective use of educational technology and the concept of Lifelong

Learning, including the recommendations of the Education Technology and the Higginson reports. The policies and strategies are wide-ranging and identify important implications for:

— college management;

— curriculum and staff development;

— access arrangements for students;

— the standardisation of ICT hardware and software resources;

— technical support;

— support for students with learning difficulties and/or disabilities;

— the monitoring and evaluation of the effectiveness of ICT in supporting students' learning.

The policies and strategies have been prepared by at least one senior manager with expertise in ICT working closely with the principal or director and other senior staff, normally through a committee established for the development of ICT across the college. Realistic targets and time scales have been set for their implementation and the roles and responsibilities of staff are clearly defined. The ICT policies and strategies are included in the CDP and are approved by the governing body. The development of suitable policies and strategies for ICT is at an early stage in about one-fifth of colleges.

Although senior management teams are setting realistic targets for the development of an ICT infrastructure, insufficient emphasis is placed on the use of ICT to support teaching and learning. Approximately one-third of colleges have not produced written policies or strategies for the development of ICT across the curriculum. As a result, there is no effective planning to use ICT to support teaching and learning, and the development of existing ICT facilities varies considerably between curriculum areas.

In addition, there is no coherent cross-college strategy to improve students access to ICT facilities and to develop suitable learning centres and the IT skills of staff and students. In particular, the needs of students with learning difficulties and/or disabilities are not assessed and met. The development of ICT in these colleges is not managed well and progress towards the implementation of an effective ICT infrastructure is poor.

Priorities for ICT have not been identified and there are no procedures to monitor the progress of the development of ICT systems. About three-quarters of colleges have established procedures, including codes of conduct, to ensure students use the ICT facilities safely and correctly. On occasions, however, there are insufficient ICT facilities to meet the needs of all students and the procedures are difficult to implement, for example, when a number of students in a class are required to share a computer system to complete a learning task and supervision is weak.

In about 25% of the colleges, students do not have clear codes of conduct when using the ICT systems. In these colleges, access is denied to students at certain times because some computer rooms are unsupervised and locked. In all colleges, there are appropriate policies for students to use and access specialist equipment such as video or satellite systems. Specialist equipment is used by students in specific vocational areas and is not normally for general use. These students are usually competent in using specialist equipment relevant to their vocational area and are provided with open access arrangements. All colleges have recognised the need to establish common standards for hardware and software. About three-quarters have managed to achieve this objective which has avoided duplication of computer systems, improved the efficiency of the technical support and, allowed the demands from individual programme areas to be planned and delivered more effectively.

The co-ordination and implementation of ICT across the curriculum is most successful in those colleges where there is strong support from senior management. In these colleges, committees for the development and use of ICT in teaching and learning have been established for senior management to work with committed staff. As a result, they have produced comprehensive written policies and strategies which are used to develop effectively ICT across the college.

Heads of schools and course co-ordinators have been consulted and have contributed significantly to the development and implementation of ICT policies and strategies within their respective programme areas. They have clearly identified the strengths and weaknesses of the current ICT provision, and clarified objectives and time scales for the implementation of ICT learning strategies within individual programmes.

The quality of the technical support for the maintenance of the ICT facilities varies considerably across and within colleges. About half of the colleges rely mainly on the non-specialist technicians to maintain the computers, together with maintenance contracts agreed with the suppliers when the ICT facilities are acquired. As a result, some ICT equipment is not always maintained in working order. About half the colleges use specialist computer technicians to maintain the ICT systems. This ensures the ICT systems are available for use.

There is, however, a significant demand from industry for specialist computer technicians and colleges find it difficult to recruit and retain them. There is a trend for colleges to adopt a policy of leasing ICT facilities to replace outdated systems quickly and cost-effectively, particularly suites of laptop computers for use in outreach centres. Maintenance contracts are included in the leasing arrangements and ensure the ICT facilities are used efficiently.

Educational reform in the United States is at an interesting, but perplexing, point in its evolution. The current wave of school reform is, in theory at least, research-based, which provides an opportunity for educational researchers, and perhaps even educators, to test new approaches. Recent developments in reading and comprehensive reform provide teachers-and their schools-with a range of choices about the types of reform strategies they may want to undertake.

However, there is a long history of failure of education reforms, especially in urban schools, which complicates efforts to develop policies and strategies to guide the choices educators might make about reform strategies. Different and potentially competing rationales have been used to argue to the new wave of reading and comprehensive reforms. This complicates efforts to evaluate the impact of education reforms. Professional development, especially providing opportunities for educators to collaborate in schools, can foster improvement in educational outcomes.

While there may be substantial disagreements about philosophies and strategies among the advocates for comprehensive reforms, they are in a coalition of advocates for comprehensive reform. Also, with reading reform, there are long-standing disputes about direct instruction, but many reforms aligned with a literature-rich philosophy benefit from the new advocacy for direct instruction, which has influenced new state and federal investments in reading reform.

While it is widely recognized that competing theories, or hypotheses, guide reform efforts, researchers seldom investigate competing rationales for reform. To achieve this goal, it is necessary to discern the assumptions made by the reform advocates, as well as to analyze data that permits an objective testing of these assumptions. This is a complicated task because most of the research on reading reforms holds implicit advocacy positions. Thus, not only is it difficult to conceptualize research in ways that make it possible to assess different assumptions about reform, but it can be even more difficult to find data that can be used to test these assumptions.

Instead of testing the rationales for reforms, most researchers conduct confirmatory research related to a specific reform model. By testing a single hypothesis rather than examining empirical evidence in relation to competing hypotheses, researchers eventually play the role of providing confirmatory evidence for individual reformers.

The professional development hypothesis essentially is that teachers need time for professional development that involves collaboration on strategies for improving educational outcomes. In the middle 1990s, the Indiana Department of Education (IDOE) initiated efforts to support professional development for teachers. Initially, they studied state policies on professional development, focusing on release time for teachers in various states. The IDOE has continued to advocate for subsidizing release time for teachers' professional development. As a second phase of their advocacy process, the IDOE commissioned a study of the research base for professional development. This study found that "successful" professional development is:

— School-based, that is, focused on particular problems of each school and selected by the teachers and principal to help address those problems.

— Followed up in teachers' classrooms by such means as peer coaching or schoolbased research and evaluation teams.

— Collaborative, so that groups of professionals at schools can work together to solve the school problems most critical to student learning.

— Embedded in the daily lives of teachers, so that they undertake professional growth as a central responsibility of teaching.

— Focused on student learning, so that teams of teachers at the school attend to the actual effects of professional development on the performance of the students for whom they are responsible.

These principles have been widely disseminated in Indiana and nationally. In Indiana, the IDOE strongly encourages schools to consider these principles whenever they submit proposals for categorical funds. Therefore the professional development rationale was embedded in the program and was integral to the funding process in EIGP. To receive a grant, a school either received a subsidy for professional development in Reading Recovery, or needed to include a focus on professional development in their grant application.

Unfortunately, few conceptual frameworks have been developed for the analysis of the effects of professional development on student outcomes. These conceptual models argue that professional development has a direct influence on professional practices and influences student outcomes as a result of changes in educational practice outcomes.

The comprehensive and cohesive reform approaches are essential to improving schools' outcomes.A comprehensive school restructuring process designed for schools with large populations at risk for learning failure. Success for All (SFA) balances a skills-oriented instructional approach with a heavy emphasis on collaboration and teamwork among educators. The program has a substantial research base mostly conducted by advocates for SFA.

Many schools in Indiana used direct approaches in their early reading instruction. Parent involvement was widely used as a strategy in early reading programs. About half of the schools used book distribution.

6

Curriculum Development in South Asia

India

The Constitution of India provides directives regarding the development of education throughout the country. The areas in which the respective central and state governments have domain have been identified in the Constitution as the central list, state list and concurrent list. Until the late 1970s, school education had been on the state list, which meant that states had the final say in the management of their respective school systems. However, in 1976, education was transferred to the concurrent list through a constitutional amendment, the objective being to promote meaningful educational partnerships between the central and state governments. Today, the central government establishes broad education policies for school curricula development and management practices. These serve as guidelines for the states.

National policies are evolved through a mechanism of extensive consultations, in which all the states and union territories actively participate. Periodically, the central/ state governments appoint commissions and committees to examine various aspects of education. In addition, countrywide debate takes place on various educational issues. The recommendations of various commissions, committees and national seminars, and the consensus that emerges during these national debates, form the basis for India's education policies.

During the post-independence period, a major concern of the Government of India and of the states was education as a factor vital to national development. In this context, India's educational reconstruction problems have been periodically reviewed by several commissions and committees. Their deliberations, recommendations and reports have formed the basis for the 1968 National Policy on Education (NPE) and the National Policy on Education Resolution of 1986.

The impact of national debates on curriculum In 1986, extensive deliberations by various national committees on the country's education system and policy culminated with the decision for a national curricular framework containing a common core along with flexible components. The common core includes the history of India's freedom movement; constitutional obligations and other content essential to nurture national identity.

These core elements are intended to cut across subject areas and were designed to promote a number of values (such as India's cultural heritage, egalitarianism, democracy, and secularism, equality of the sexes, protection of the environment, removal of social barriers, observance of the small-family norm and inculcation of the scientific approach). Also, in order to reinforce the view that the whole world is one family, the curriculum would have the objective to promote international cooperation and peaceful coexistence.

With regard to reorientation of educational content and processes, the NPE emphasized the need for bridging the schism between the formal education system and the country's rich and varied cultural traditions. To this end, the preoccupation with modern technologies must not be allowed to sever new generations' ties to India's history and culture. In view of the growing concern over the erosion of essential values and increasing cynicism in society, readjustments in the curriculum are to be carried out so that education becomes a forceful tool for the cultivation of social and moral values. The policy further emphasized the integral role that manual work, sports and physical education should play in the learning process and the need to strengthen science and mathematics education.

The process of curriculum development in India lies between the two extremes of centralization and decentralization. From time to time, the national government formulates the National Policy on Education which includes broad guidelines regarding content and process of education at different stages. These guidelines are further elaborated by the National Council of Educational Research and Training (NCERT).

Using as its foundation the NPEs of 1968 and 1986, two curriculum initiatives have been launched by NCERT:

(a) The Curriculum for the Ten-Year School: A framework (1975); and

(b) The National Curriculum for Elementary and Secondary Education: A framework (1988).

The curriculum framework prepared at the central level provides a broad overview of the school curriculum, including general objectives, subject-wise objectives, suggested scheme of studies, and guidelines for the transaction of the curriculum and the evaluation of pupil outcomes.

These detailed curricula, syllabi and instructional materials are developed at the national level. The NCERT has also developed the syllabi and instructional materials used in the schools run by central organizations. However, the states consider whether to adopt or adapt the NCERT syllabi and instructional materials.

Thus, the NCERT curriculum framework is always a suggestion rather than prescriptive and it is not enforceable by law in the states. However, it is readily accepted by the states because of the NCERT's credibility and the participatory development approach it follows.

The National Curriculum

The following social, cultural, political, economic and educational parameters have guided the development of the national curriculum framework:

— All citizens of India should have equal access to education. The specific needs of the disadvantaged sections of the society ought to be met through the curriculum;

— Education regarding India's cultural heritage needs to be imparted to students in order to develop national identity and a spirit of togetherness;

— It is essential to impart knowledge of the citizens' duties and rights, and ideals of the Constitution of India to children;

— In view of the erosion of values, it is imperative through the curriculum to inculcate moral and social values amongst students;

— Besides national identity and unity, it is also imperative to develop international understanding through the curriculum;

— Protection of the environment and conservation of natural resources should be major objectives of school curriculum;

— In view of the increasing population of the country, it is imperative to include suitable content relating to population education in the syllabi of different subjects;

— The curriculum should aim at preparing a child for life, which means that relevant knowledge should be imparted and appropriate skills, competencies and values developed;

— Education plays a significant role in national development by increasing human resources. Therefore, the primary objective of the curriculum ought to be total development of the child's personality;

— All the processes of education should be child-centred, with the teacher playing the role of a facilitator during the process of learning;

— The curriculum should aim at developing students' creative potential;

— The curriculum should develop a scientific approach amongst students;

— 'Work should not be considered as distinct from education. Instead , work should be adopted as a medium for imparting education;

— The process of evaluation should be continuous and comprehensive;

— Media and educational technology ought to be employed to make the transactions of curriculum effective.

An important development since the National Policy on Education was formulated in 1986 has been the acceptance across the country of a common structure of education and the introduction by most states of the 10+2+3 system. There are eight years of elementary education (five years of primary school and three years of upper primary/ middle schooling) and four years of secondary education (two years of general secondary and two years of higher secondary).

The education system seeks to give due recognition and importance to the social organization, traditions, customs and value systems of the various communities, particularly Scheduled Castes and Scheduled Tribes. This is supported among other ways by the development of materials and curricula in their languages.

General education

The national curriculum envisages the first ten years of school as the period of general education and that the diversified curriculum should be introduced at the end of general education (i.e. at the beginning of the senior secondary stage.) This plan provides all students with an opportunity to receive instruction in each of the curricular areas considered essential for their overall development.

Undifferentiated curricula

The national curriculum framework also envisages an undifferentiated curriculum for all children irrespective of sex and place of residence (i.e. urban or rural).

Minimum levels of learning

The 1986 NPE recommended the establishment of minimum levels of learning (MLLs) for the various subject areas at the different school stages. In this context, a Government of India committee (under the Chairmanship of Professor R.H. Dave) elaborated the MLL curriculum concept that designates the competencies to be mastered by the primary level pupils in each subject, at specific points in time.

For the first five years of primary schooling, the MLL covers the mother tongue, mathematics, social science and science. The MLL approach implies that the teacher's responsibility is not confined to syllabus coverage. Rather, teachers must be responsible for their pupils mastering designated competencies.

This approach has necessitated ongoing development of MLL-based textbooks and MLL-based evaluation. It has also introduced a higher concept of teacher accountability. Teachers are now held responsible for pupil competency development and not merely for teaching the prescribed syllabus as was the previous practice.

Commoncore elements

The 1988 National Curriculum Framework (NCF) recommended compulsory core curriculum elements to be taught throughout the country. Most of these core elements are aimed at the development of national identity and a spirit of togetherness leading to national unity.

The common core elements recommended in the NCF are: the history of India's freedom struggle; constitutional obligations; content essential for the development of national identity; common cultural heritage of India; democracy, secularism, socialism; gender equality; environmental conservation; removal of social barriers; the small-family norm; and development of a scientific approach.

The core elements are not to be treated as separate subject areas. Rather, the content is to be interwoven into the different subject areas. Here, it should be noted that, for the first time during India's post-independence period, conscious efforts have been made to place values at the centre stage of curriculum.

Continuous and comprehensive evaluation

The NCF also considered the limitations of the existing evaluation system, which relies mostly on one-shot, end-of- the-year impact evaluation. This annual examination measures skills attainment and the affective domain is generally ignored (i.e. attitudes development). To remedy this, the NCF recommended that evaluation should be treated as an integral part of the classroom teaching/ learning process. Furthermore, evaluation, conducted periodically, should provide the type of feedback on student achievement that enables teachers to improve their methodology, if required.

Interactive teaching

It is recognized that both the educational curriculum content and process must be reoriented in order to bring about overall quality improvement. During the past few years, successful attempts have been made to reorient the educational content to current development and demands of both society and the different disciplines. However, this initiative has not been accompanied by a corresponding change in the modes of curriculum transaction, which remains predominantly one of verbal exposition by the teacher. The expository style of teaching, involving mostly oneway communication, puts the learner in the role of a passive recipient—a mere object of education.

This situation is not conducive to the development of creative, critical and analytical thinking by students. An interactive teaching methodology involving continuing dialogue between the teacher and pupils (discussion, investigation, problemsolving, etc.) could provide an educational environment more conducive to developing certain abstract cognitive skills.

Scheme of studies

The 1988 National Curriculum Framework has recommended the areas shown in Table 1, along with the appropriate time weightage at the upper primary and secondary levels:

Table 1
The National Curriculum Framework

Upper primary stage	Time weightage (%)
Three languages	32
Mathematics	12
Social science	12
Science	12
Health and physical education	10
Arts	10
Work experience	10
Secondary stage	
Three languages	30
Mathematics	13
Social science	13
Science	13
Work experience	13
Health and physical education	9
Arts	9

Languages

The NCF envisages the study of three languages at the upper primary and secondary stages: first, the mother tongue/regional language; second, Hindi or English (in the case of non-Hindi-speaking states); and third, one of the modern Indian languages (English in Hindi- speaking states; Hindi or English in non-Hindi-speaking states).

Mathematics

Functional mathematics are taught at the upper primary stage; arithmetic, including commercial mathematics, should be completed, to a very large extent, by the end of the upper primary stage. The secondary stage begins the transition from functional mathematics to the study of mathematics as a discipline.

Science

The upper primary science teaching objectives are to develop an understanding of the nature of scientific knowledge; and certain physical, chemical, biological principles and their relationship to the operation of scientific principles in nature, as well as in daily life. The aim of the teaching of science at the secondary level is focused on problem-solving and decision making through the learning of key concepts, which cut across all the science disciplines.

Social sciences

The study of social sciences at the upper primary stage is

comprized of the study of history, geography, civics and contemporary issues and problems. At the secondary stage, it incorporates elements of history, geography, civics and economics to promote an understanding of contemporary India.

Arts

The aim of art education is learner sensitization to the beauty in line, colour, form, movement and sound. The upper primary programme incorporates:

(i) drawing, painting, printing, collage, clay modelling, puppet construction;

(ii) free expression artistic creation;

(iii) handling of simple musical instruments;

(iv) movement, mime, simple dance forms, community singing;

(v) simple concepts of visual and performing arts;

(vi) stories of great personalities in the field of arts, and stories connected with other countries.

At the secondary stage, it incorporates:

(i) study and exploration of visual and aural resources;

(ii) projects leading to creative visual and aural forms;

(iii) intergroup, interschool art activities;

(iv) study groups, interaction with community artists;

(v) exploration of community/neighbourhood traditional art forms.

Health and physical education

This area focuses on the holistic health of the learner and the community, thereby establishing the important place of mental and emotional, as well as physical health. The first ten years of content focuses on general promotion of healthful living as well as on major health problems of the country. In physical education, sports and games, the emphasis is given to indigenous traditional games. As a system which promotes the integral development of body and mind, yoga receives special attention.

Morals and values

These areas are treated as an integral curriculum component for which all teachers are responsible. Work experience. The work experience incorporates purposive, manual work resulting in either goods or services useful to the community. It is an essential component at all stages of education and is to be provided through wellstructured, graded programmes. At both the upper primary and secondary stages, work experience emphasizes agricultural and technological processes to facilitate the integration of science, mathematics and technology into community life.

Statelevel curriculum implementation

The available feedback from the states indicates that, for the most part, they have revised their curricula along the lines recommended by the 1986 NPE and 1988 NCF. However, several have made adjustments that respond to specific local needs or sociopolitical pressures. Following are some highlights that reflect the dynamics of curriculum implementation at the state level.

Languages

All states (except Tamil Nadu) have adopted the three-language formula. Although it was envisaged that only one language (mother tongue or regional language) would be taught at the primary stage, many states have taken the initiative and introduced a second and third language at this level.

For example, Punjab state recently decided to introduce English, along with the regional language in class I. In the state of Sikkim, English is taught as a subject and used as the medium of instruction beginning right from class I. The policy of using English as the medium of instruction beginning in class I is being implemented in almost all the private, unaided schools throughout the country.

Another interesting variation encompasses classical language teaching—an area that the NCF did not address. Most of the Hindi-speaking states, and even central school organizations, have made provisions for teaching Sanskrit as a third language.

In fact, to accommodate the study of Sanskrit along with other languages, some states have even made provisions for the teaching of a fourth language. (In Uttar Pradesh, Sanskrit is compulsory and taught as part of Hindi.) It would appear that Sanskrit is in demand because it is associated with ancient Indian culture and is the mother to many modern Indian languages.

Other scholastic areas

Several states have modified the NCF science and social sciences recommendations. For example, in place of the integrated science approach, they have opted for the single- subject discipline approach. West Bengal has made provisions for the teaching of history and geography only at the upper primary stage.

Non-scholastic areas

In India, work experience, arts, and health and physical education are generally categorized as non-scholastic areas. The curriculum framework has emphasized that these areas are essential for all around development of the child's personality. However, being non-examination subjects, these areas are not taken seriously by the teachers and students.

In some states, arts has not been made a compulsory subject at the secondary stage. In the states and schools where arts is a compulsory or optional area, only the visual arts are taught. Performance arts like music and dance are taught only in a limited number of schools. In the states of Punjab, Haryana and Himachal Pradesh, arts has been clustered with home science and agriculture and the students have been given the option to choose any one of these areas.

Values education

The NCF also envisaged that values education should permeate all aspects of school life and, therefore, should be integrated into all the curriculum areas. However, states like Haryana, Goa, Himachal Pradesh, Karnataka, Punjab, Sikkim, Tamil Nadu, Andhra Pradesh and Uttar Pradesh have all introduced moral education or moral science as independent subject areas, with distinct time allocations.

Apparently, this has occurred in the light of pleas that, given the progressive weakening of the moral fabric of society, the integrated approach does not provide values education with the prominent place it deserves.

Competency-based textbooks

After the identification of MLL (minimum levels of learning), introductory advocacy programmes were launched to promote the concept as an approach to curriculum development, teaching and learning and pupil evaluation. A number of states have since produced primary-stage competency- based textbooks in different curricular areas.

Curriculum Outcomes

The Government of India found it necessary to appoint a National Advisory Committee (NAC) to look into frequent complaints about the excessive burden of the curriculum on children. The NAC submitted report findings in 1993. This report, which took note of the widespread perception regarding the heavy load of the school curriculum, also identified the roots of the problem: inability to distinguish between information and knowledge; society's competitive social ethos; the desire to catch up with developed countries; centralized curriculum development processes; non-participation of teachers in the various curriculum development processes; excessive dependence on experts; incomprehensibility of textbooks; and absence of an academic ethos in schools.

The committee further determined that the academic burden perception is tied to in comprehension, a problem which can be addressed (to some extent) by modifying the curriculum development goals, as well as the textbook writing process and by improving the school environment by providing the required infrastructure.

Most of the NAC recommendations were accepted by the Government. All state governments were asked to initiate appropriate follow-up measures to implement the recommendations of the committee, including review of curriculum and textbooks.

Evaluation of textbooks

The textbooks used in different states and union territories are already subject to periodic evaluation. They are reviewed from the perspective of national integration—the objective being to promote peace and harmony in the country and enable children to learn to live together with people of different religious, linguistic, ethnic and cultural groups.

During these reviews any content deemed to have a secular bias or to be destructive to national unity is identified and recommended for removal. Textbooks are also continuously evaluated from the standpoint of gender, scientific temper and relevance, etc.

Improving quality of curriculum transaction

NCERT, the Central Board of Secondary Education (CBSE), the State Councils of Educational Research and Training (SCERTS) and the State Boards of Secondary Education have initiated a number of projects to improve the quality of curriculum transmission in schools.

To improve the quality of mathematics education, CBSE has launched the project Operation Mathematics emphasizing the reorientation of all teachers. The CBSE has also developed source materials in the education areas of: environment, values, consumer and population. Furthermore, a network of training institutions has been established in the country to enhance teacher competencies through in-service education.

Emerging trends in curriculum development

In the light of changing societal needs and aspirations, certain high demand-driven areas are likely to have an impact on the school curriculum. It appears that, among other areas, language education, values education and information technology shall be matters of serious debate in the next cycle of curriculum renewal. Art education is also scheduled for reform in the next cycle of curriculum renewal.

Language education

The introduction of English at the primary stage is one of the demands which school systems are finding difficult to resist. Perhaps this demand is based on the assumption that the study of English can give children an edge in a highly competitive society.

Values education

After the establishment of a National Commission for Human Rights, momentum has been gathering for incorporating this area into the school curriculum. The interim report issued by Justice Verma's Committee (on the fundamental duties of citizens) strongly recommended that fundamental duties should be incorporated at all stages of the school curriculum, as well as into different teacher-education programmes.

The incorporation of human rights and citizens' fundamental duties into the curriculum can help pupils learn to live together, one of the four pillars of learning identified by the International Commission on Education in the Twenty-first Century.

Computer education

Computer education is expected to soon occupy a prominent space in India's school curriculum, it being recognized that, in the information age, skills in the use of these technologies are invaluable.

Bangladesh

The Government of Bangladesh recognizes that education is an important prerequisite for ensuring sustainable development. The country's constitution obligates the State to provide basic education to citizens and eradicate illiteracy within a given time frame.

As a signatory to the World Conference on Education For All; World Conference on Children's Rights; and the EFA Summit Conference of Nine High-

Population Countries, Bangladesh is committed to the eradication of illiteracy by the year 2006.

As a result of both government and private efforts over the last two decades, some important improvements have occurred in the primary education sector. More than 95% of children aged 6 to 10 years are admitted to primary schools and the dropout rate is now only 38%. The literacy rate for the population over 15 currently stands at 56%, in comparison to 1971 post-liberation figures reflecting a rate of only 22% for that same group. During the past twenty-five years, considerable improvements have also taken place in secondary education.

However, although Bangladesh has experienced quantitative educational improvement, the qualitative aspects of education have become a cause of government concern. Steps have been taken to address educational quality and it is in this larger context that curriculum has come to play a crucial role.

In order to place in proper perspective some of the key issues and actions taken to improve educational quality, a brief overview of primary and secondary education structures and of curriculum development is provided below.

The current five years for completing primary education is an insufficient amount of time for students to obtain the requisite level of literacy, knowledge, abilities, attitudes and values for solving the problems of everyday life.

The New Education Policy, which has yet to be implemented, recommends that primary education be increased from five to eight years in order to enable students to attain minimum ability levels and the capacity for lifelong learning.

A number of different institutions of primary education exist including: kindergarten, general primary, Ebtadayee Madrasah and non-governmental organization schools. The standards and characteristics of these schools vary. Thus, from the very outset, differences in children's abilities, attitudes and values are created. It has become mandatory to eliminate these existing educational disparities and to introduce a common system of education.

Currently, approximately 78,000 primary schools are subsumed under ten or eleven distinct categories. The following tables provide an overview of the current situation.

Beginning in May 1986, the Government decided to merge the primary school classes I and II and, concurrently, to introduce a liberal promotion policy as part of the effort to further reduce dropout rates.

With this liberalized policy, promotion from classes I to II and from classes II to III became automatic. However, assessment of pupils' performance is still supposed to occur throughout the year.

Table 2
Bangladesh primary education institutional enrolment

Year	Total	Boys	Girls
1990	12,051,172	6,662,427	5,388,745
1991	12,635,419	6,910,092	5,725,328
1992	13,017,270	7,048,542	5,968,728
1993	14,067,332	7,525,862	6,541,470

1994	15,180,680	8,084,117	7,132,668
1995	17,284,157	9,094,489	8,189,668
1996	17,580,416	9,219,358	8,361,058
1997	18,031,673	9,364,899	8,666,774

Table 3

Bangladesh primary education enrolment by gender (%)

Year	Boys	Girls
1990	55.28	44.72
1991	54.69	45.31
1992	54.15	45.85
1993	53.50	46.50
1994	53.02	46.98
1995	52.62	47.38
1996	52.44	47.56
1997	51.94	48.06

Table 4

Bangladesh primary education dropout rate (% of total enrolment)

Year	*Rate*
1991	59.30
1992	46.60
1993	39.60
1994	38.70
1995	38.00

Secondary Education

The present secondary education system in Bangladesh

encompasses grade levels 6 to 12. Most secondary schools are private. In 1996, only 3.6% of the total number of recognized schools were government schools. Secondary education is divided into three stages: junior secondary (classes VI and VII); secondary (classes IX and X); and higher secondary (classes XI and XII).

Higher secondary schools can be intermediate colleges or degree colleges. A significant increase (16.4%) in the total number of secondary institutions occurred between 1995 and 1996, with secondary and higher secondary schools accounting for most of the increase. Noteworthy progress in some areas and stagnation in others characterize secondary education in Bangladesh. Significant progress has been made in improving enrolment, especially among females.

Programmes encouraging the enrolment of girls in secondary education have had a profoundly positive effect, with an increase in enrolment from 31.9% in 1991 to 45.6% in 1996. However, in contrast, transition, attendance, completion and pass rates remain low.

In 1995, 78% of the students completing class V went on to enrol in class VI. The average secondary school attendance rate was about 60%. Completion rates for classes VI to X improved, reaching 56.4% in 1995, in comparison to 48% in 1991. However, these figures belie a highly inefficient system, with dropout rates remaining high and pass rates in final exams declining.

For example, in 1995, the estimated dropout rates for classes VI to X and classes XI and XII, respectively, were 43.6% (49% for girls) and 38% (36% for girls). In 1997, the pass rate for the class X Secondary School Certificate Examination (SSC) was only 52.14%, compared to 64.95% in 1991. For the class XII Higher Secondary Certification

Examination (LISC), the 1997 rate of 52.14% was down from a high of 64.95% in 1991. Furthermore, only 15.8% of the junior secondary school and 36.7% of secondary school teachers have professional qualifications.

With a view to increasing women's participation at secondary level, the Government, the Norwegian Overseas Development Agency (NORAD), the Asian Development Bank (ADB) and the World Bank are supporting stipends for female students. This programme has served to increase the enrolment of women in secondary education institutions.

Curriculum Development in Bangladesh

In 1982, the National Curriculum Development Centre merged with the Textbook Board to form the National Curriculum and Textbook Board (NCTB). The NCTB currently serves as the national curriculum agency for the country as a whole and has been entrusted with curriculum and instructional materials development activities from pre-primary to pre-university level. The tasks of the National Curriculum and Textbook Board include:

- completion of curriculum revision for all primary grades;
- field trials as well as the production of teaching-learning materials for classes I-V, including pupil assessment schemes;
- revision of the curriculum in education and the curriculum for pre-service education and training of primary school teachers;

- introduction of revised curriculum and materials for classes I-V in the school system throughout the country;
- development of supplementary/complementary teaching aids (i.e. charts, maps, reading-learning materials, kits, video films, etc.);
- organization of experimental and innovative activities in the content of primary education;
- development of the capacity to address women's development issues;
- provision of technical support to other institutions in developing curriculum and establishing linkages between formal, non-formal, religious education streams;
- development of training packages and participation in the training programmes for dissemination of revised primary curriculum;
- monitoring and evaluation of the training programme and development of reinforcement materials;
- development of motivational materials for media coverage;
- revision of Junior Secondary Curriculum and materials in line with the revised primary curriculum and field trials;
- review of existing secondary curriculum and development of a plan of action for modification.

During the Third Five-Year Plan (1985-90), the NCTB undertook comprehensive curriculum renewal and modification activities in the area of primary education.

The main thrust of this activity was to restructure and reform the primary curriculum to meet the demands of universal compulsory primary education, with particular focus on qualitative improvement.

The outcome was a competency-based primary school curriculum comprised of fifty-three terminal competencies to be achieved by all primary school pupils who successfully complete the five-year primary education cycle.

In this context, the following have been developed: detailed syllabi for eleven subject areas of grades I and II; a trial edition of textbooks; teacher source books; and a continuous pupil assessment scheme, along with a register for keeping assessment records.

Improvement of curricula has been undertaken with the help of foreign and domestic experts. Steps have been taken to train teachers to be able to use new materials with understanding and skill, with a view to preparing them to introduce the competency based curriculum.

The curriculum emphasizes mastery learning supported by diagnosis of pupils learning difficulties, followed by remedial instruction, appropriate teaching-learning strategies, revised instructional materials, and tools and techniques for continuous assessment of pupil performance.

The new curriculum was implemented during the Fourth Five-Year Plan (1990-95), with new approaches towards the evaluation of pupils' achievements.

The primary level curriculum has been formulated on the basis of Bangladesh's socioeconomic situation, as well as the children's physical and mental make-up and their cultural awareness. Subjects in primary level include

Bangla (the mother tongue), mathematics and environmental studies, social studies, science, arts and crafts, physical education, music.

English language and religious studies (with emphasis on the ways of life and moral education) will be introduced in class III. Classes VI to VIII will be gradually incorporated under primary education. At these levels, the subjects to be studied will be Bangla, mathematics, general science, social studies (Islam, Hinduism, Buddhism, Christianity), multi-disciplinary learning (home economics, agriculture, etc.), religion, fine arts, health and physical education.

The present curriculum at the primary as well as junior secondary and secondary stages contains elements of population education, including information on the socioeconomic impact of the population explosion. The content has been incorporated into the textbooks of classes III to X.

The average amount of weekly teaching hours in each grade at primary level is three hours for Bangla; three hours for mathematics; thirty minutes for music, arts and crafts, and physical education; and two-and-a-half hours for all the other subjects. The medium of instruction is Bangla (mother tongue).

In the present curriculum, summative assessment (in the form of an annual examination in each grade) has been abandoned. Instead, a system of continuous pupil assessment has been introduced.

The system requires teachers to assess students regularly for every competency acquired in a particular lesson (through observation, oral/written assessment) and to record achievement on a monthly basis using three scales (namely grades A, B and C).

For grades I-II, all the students get promoted to the next classes, and for grades III-V, promotions are given on the basis of students' achievement. No certificate is awarded after completion of the five-year primary schooling, but a scholarship examination is held annually for 20% of the students of grade 5—on the basis of which scholarships are awarded to successful students.

Curriculum Development at the Secondary Level

Under the Secondary Education Development Project of the ADB, the junior secondary school curriculum has been revised and materials prepared on the basis of competencies identified for this stage of education; approximately 150,000 teachers have received short-term training in the new curriculum; ten teacher-training colleges have been upgraded; and pre-service and in-service training programmes have been conducted.

Under the ADB Higher Secondary Education Project, five new higher teacher-training institutes are being established. During 1996-98, the secondary and higher secondary curricula were revised and implemented and textbooks prepared. The monitoring and evaluation systems have been improved and implemented.

Curriculum Development: Areas for Improvement

Some of the major deficiencies in curriculum development in Bangladesh include:

(a) lack of professional expertise in the development of modern curriculum, both in the NCTB and nationally;

(b) lack of a solid research base providing assessment information about the previous curriculum and the areas needing revision; and

(c) insufficient curriculum emphasis on such competencies as understanding, comprehension and application.

Although the three stages of secondary education form part of a concentric curriculum development, during the actual development process there was little coordination between these stages.

In fact, the greatest part of the work was carried out for the junior secondary stage, and then subsequently reviewed in each of the other stages where attempts were made to address areas of weak emphasis by adding content.

Another problem is the absence of a system of ongoing curriculum review. The syllabus standing committee system within NCTB is not operational. The curriculum section staff should be monitoring the curriculum and textbooks usage and effectiveness in the teaching situation in order to ensure that they are up-to-date and relevant. Unfortunately, at present, this important work is not being done.

The establishment of a curriculum research section is urgently needed for effective curriculum development. The issues affecting the impact of curriculum change in the classroom need to be assessed objectively.

Without this research base, curriculum development will continue to be based largely on ad hoc decisions resulting from the views of persons who often lack first-hand knowledge of the overcrowded and poor conditions in most schools.

The staff of such a research section will require training and support, as well as increased resources, in order to perform regular classroom visits and assessments.

Lack of expertise is also a fundamental problem. Reviews of the capacity of the NCTB by different institutions in Bangladesh have repeatedly highlighted the lack of trained professional curriculum developers.

Although growth in the primary and secondary education sectors in Bangladesh is quite satisfactory, the quality of education is not. However, the country is striving hard to achieve this quality and, in this context, many efforts have been undertaken with the help of domestic and expatriate experts to improve the curriculum.

Bhutan

The kingdom of Bhutan is a mountainous, Buddhist country with an area of roughly 46,000 square kilometres, located between China in the north and India in the south. It has been an independent nation throughout its history, although it was only in the seventeenth century that Zhabdrung Ngawang Namgyel (1594-1652) unified it into one nation-state. The present King, His Majesty Druk Oyalpo Jigme Singye Wangchuck, is the fourth monarch to rule the country.

Prior to the year 1920, monastic education, which included the study of Buddhist religion, liturgy, philosophy, astrology and the fine arts (painting, sculpture, music and dance), was the only form of formal education available in the country. The first modern school was established in 1920. Modernization in Bhutan, however, can be said to have begun only in 1961 with the launching of the Five-Year Development Plan (1961-65). From the outset of the planned development, the number of schools in Bhutan increased to fifty-nine (twenty-nine private and thirty governmental) and a Department of Education was established. With the creation of this institution, the private schools were converted into governmental schools, thereby establishing a centralized and uniform system of education which has largely continued until today, although a few private schools have been opened lately following government encouragement.

With the Royal Government's heavy investment on education during the Five-Year Development Plans, within a period of three and half decades, Bhutan has been able to create a modern education system from primary to tertiary levels. Enrolment at all levels has grown considerably over the years as a result of the government's commitment to education. By 1998, the total number of students reached 100,355 .

The present pre-tertiary educational structure consists of nine years of basic education, comprising one year pre-primary, six years primary, and two years junior high, followed by four years of secondary education comprising two years of high school and two years of higher secondary level. Access from one level to the other is merit-based and determined by the national and external examinations, as well as by the human resource plans and the space available at the relevant levels of education.

The National Institute of Education (NIE) offers a three-year Bachelor of Education degree course for grade

XII graduates and a one-year teacher training programme—Post-Graduate Certificate in Education (PGCE)—for candidates who already have a Bachelor's Degree either in humanities, commerce or science. The two-year Primary Teacher's Certificate (PTC) course is offered for the grade X graduates at the NIE, as well as the Teacher-Training College (TTC) in Paro. NIE has also started a Distance Education Programme for primary teachers since 1995. An eighteen-month training programme for Dzongkha (national language) teachers is also offered by the Teacher-Training College, Paro. Education has always been provided free of charge from primary to tertiary level. This includes not only free tuition, but also the provision of textbooks, stationery, meals and boarding facilities where required.

The Curriculum

The school curriculum until the mid-1980s was imported from India and all the teaching materials were those prescribed for Anglo-Indian schools, except for Dzongkha. From the mid-1980s, the then Education Department started Bhutanizing the education system so that teaching and learning in schools was in accordance with national needs and aspirations. The development of a relevant curriculum and curriculum materials for schools throughout the country began following this important policy change.

The first big curricular change came with the introduction of the New Approach to Primary Education (NAPE) project which emphasized activity-based learning, shifting the focus from 'teacher-centredness to child-centredness, as well as from remoteness of content to familiarity of content' (Dolkar, 1995).

The next big change was the introduction of Bhutanese history and geography for grades 6-8 in 1990, and then for grades 9-10 in 1993, whereby students are expected to acquire knowledge, skills, values and attitudes through this change in order to 'develop pride in being Bhutanese; ... a sense of self-discipline and duty; ... spiritual, cultural and traditional values and so contribute to national and social cohesion' (National Education Policy, 1984). Changes have also been brought about in the other school subjects.

Main Organisations Involved in Adapting Currucula

The adaptation of curricula takes place at various levels in the country. A brief discussion of the agencies involved is presented here.

Central level

Since all educational institutions are government-financed, educational programmes are largely controlled from the centre. The task of initiating and implementing all educational programmes in the country (in line with national educational policies) is entrusted to the Ministry of Health and Education (MHE) and the Education Division (ED) via its various sections. The Curriculum and Professional Support Section (CAPSS), Educational and Monitoring Support Section (EMSS), Bhutan Board of Examination (BBE), Non-Formal Education Section (NFES) and Youth Guidance and Counselling Section (YGCS) are the key existing professional bodies that are extensively involved in adapting curricula.

Curriculum and Professional Support Section (CAPSS)

When the Department of Education (subsequently the Education Division) within the Ministry of Health and Education launched the programme of Bhutanization of the education system in the mid-1980s, a Curriculum and Textbook Development Division (CTDD) was created to develop curriculum and curriculum materials for schools. However, in 1994, the practice of curriculum development had evolved to the point whereby a committee of experienced educators and teachers (formed from various subject committees) took over the implementation. With this development, the CTDD was transformed into the currently existing CAPSS, now the main body involved in curriculum research and development for the formal school system. CAPSS is staffed by curriculum officers, headed by a Director and a Deputy Director, who are responsible for each subject.

The main functions of CAPSS are:

- carrying out curriculum research and development;
- developing and writing syllabi, textbooks and manuals for grades PP-WI in all subjects;
- developing syllabi and textbooks for grades IX and X in consultation with BBE and ISCE Board, Delhi;
- training of teachers and pilot testing, evaluating, monitoring and revising curriculum materials; and
- conducting in-service workshops for teachers in different subject areas.

For the development of curriculum guidelines and materials at CAPSS, each subject unit has a subject committee (composed of members from various sections, training institutes and schools) with each unit's coordinator at CAPSS as the member-secretary. All innovations and changes in the curriculum and curriculum materials 'are discussed in the subject committee meetings, usually held twice a year. Proposals for initiating the innovations or changes are developed in consultation with the Director and Deputy Director, CAPSS, for further submission to the CAPPS Board, which meets once a year. The CAPSS Board comprises of the Director of Education as the Chairperson, all the section heads of the Education Division, Chairpersons of the various subject committees, the principal of the college, directors of the teacher-training institutes, one principal representing the high schools, and the Director of CAPSS as the member-secretary.

Once the proposal is approved, the curriculum officers of the subject units coordinate the work, involving subject committee members, subject specialists from the other sections, teacher-training institutes and schools. In terms of developing textbooks, CAPSS has started commissioning authors whose work is nevertheless closely monitored by the particular subject coordinator at CAPSS.

All the new materials that are developed also need formal approval of the Board before being printed and supplied to schools for implementation. The new materials are also reviewed by schools and by the committee members prior to the submission to the CAPSS Board. CAPSS is also responsible for publishing all curriculum materials.

Bhutan Board of Examination (BBE)

BBE is mainly responsible for organizing and conducting

all national examinations for grades VI, VIII and X, Primary Teachers' Certificate Examination and Rigshung—grades X and XII. BBE also conducts workshops for teachers on principles and techniques of assessment and evaluation and is involved in developing general guidelines for assessment with the CAPSS. The subject specialists in BBE are also members of the various subject committees.

Education Monitoring and Support Section (EMSS)

EMSS is mainly responsible for reporting on the general quality of education in schools. It monitors compliance with the national education guidelines and reports on the overall school effectiveness in relation to student achievement. This involves reviewing and evaluating school management, maintenance practices, curriculum practices, students' achievement and identification of good teaching practices as well as barriers to learning. EMSS is involved in providing necessary professional support to the District Education Officers and schools on a regular basis through forums such as Dzongkha Based In-service Programmes and School Based In-service Programmes. Some of the officers in EMSS are also members of various subject committees.

Youth Guidance and Counselling Section (YGCS)

YGCS is involved in developing and implementing a range of co-curricular and extracurricular programmes and activities, including Career Education and Guidance Programme, Scout Programme, Adolescent Health Education and Counselling Programme.

Non-Formal Education Section (NFES)

NFES is mainly responsible for launching literacy and relevant life-skill programmes for school dropouts and adults. Its main functions are:

— developing and publishing NFE learning materials;

— training NFE teachers;

— helping districts establish NFE and community learning centres; and 1 monitoring NFE programmes and recommending policies.

Technical and Vocational Education Section (TVES)

TVES plans, coordinates and monitors technical and vocational training programmes. It ensures relevant vocational skills are included in the school learning process and promotes positive attitudes among students regarding technical vocations.

Teacher-training institutes

The two teacher-training institutes, the National Institute of Education and the Teacher- Training College, take an active part in adapting curricula through pre-service and in-service teacher training. This is done by: exposing them to various approaches of teaching and learning; assisting them in developing teaching materials from the available resources; equipping them with the necessary skills and teaching techniques; and assessment and evaluation of the teaching/ learning process and the achievement of the students. Both institutes graduate 100 to 150 teachers every year for the primary and secondary schools. The lecturers of the institutes are also involved in the design and implementation of the curriculum as many of them are also members of the various subject committees. They also play an active role in organizing and conducting various in-service curriculum-related workshops for the teachers in the country every year.

District level

At the district level, the District Education Officers (DEOs) interpret for the benefit of the schools the aims and objectives and the curriculum directives from the Education Division. They provide academic and non-academic supervision, organize teacher and school development activities, monitor development activities and assist with school-based in-service programmes by visiting the schools regularly. They also support schools in obtaining teachers and resources, and developing the school infrastructure.

School level

At the school level, the head-teachers and teachers interpret the aims and objectives of education through the curriculum. They develop work schemes, lesson plans and teaching materials and practise different methodologies. Teachers also organize various types of co-curricular activities to provide pupils with balanced education. They carry out continuous assessment of the students' performance and set internal tests and examinations. They organize school-based in-service programmes to improve their classroom practices. Many teachers are also involved in developing curriculum materials at the centre and during resource national-based in-service workshops.

Problems in Adapting Curriculum in Bhutan

Curriculum specialists in Bhutan face several problems, which are largely due to the short space of time in which the modern system of education has evolved. Discussion will be limited to the main problems faced in the design, implementation and follow up of reforms.

Curriculum design

The first main problem is the lack of expertise in curriculum development. There is not much scope for consultation nor the required support and guidance. Curriculum developers are left to cope on their own with their often limited knowledge in the area. Outside experts are often invited to guide and assist, but, in many cases, their expertise and inputs are not relevant to the country's needs and situation. Valid and relevant comments for improvement are rarely received from the field. This largely affects the quality, clarity and appropriateness of the curriculum design. Lack of resources and access to quality innovations due to financial constraints are other major problems. This limits curriculum developers' access to the wealth of information and ideas on curriculum design that are available in other counties.

Insufficient time for carrying out proper situational analysis and research is another major problem. Final decisions are largely top down (from the administrators who look for immediate action and quick outcomes), leaving staff with no choice but to design the curriculum within the set time frame, which in most cases is inadequate. The problem is further exacerbated by inadequate staffing, since the curriculum developer has other commitments and cannot devote adequate time to curriculum design. This scenario, however, is rapidly changing with more people becoming specialized in curriculum development and change, thus creating more opportunities for educators to enhance their professional development. With their inputs, education in Bhutan is becoming more relevant and appropriate to the needs of the learners.

Problems in the implementation of the curriculum

As with the design process, time and resource constraints (both human and material) are the major problem. Because of the requirement for speedy implementation, inadequate time is allotted for pilot-testing the reforms in terms of their relevance and appropriateness, for carrying out a detailed plan of implementation, and for organizing resources. Furthermore, teachers hardly have the required time for preparation, the shortage of schoolteachers being a perennial problem in the system.

More support materials are needed for effective implementation. Teachers do not have much access to reference materials, except basic school textbooks. Specialists cannot offer much support to the teachers during the implementation of reforms, since they cannot visit schools regularly due to busy schedules. Thus, in most cases, the initial orientation workshop held in the beginning to familiarize teachers with the reforms and their implementation is the only support and guidance that they receive. Under such circumstances, teachers maintain their old ways of teaching, with which they feel more secure, and new reforms are hardly implemented.

Lack of proper coordination among the various sections in the centre, and with the districts and schools, is another problem faced in implementation. Teachers who receive initial training in implementing the reforms are sometimes subsequently given a new assignment or transferred to another school, resulting in the changes not being introduced.

The education system, being examination-oriented also inhibits effective implementation of the curriculum as teaching time is restricted to covering the syllabus in time for the examinations. The deployment policy of the Education Division can be seen as an additional problem. Very often the teachers who have graduated from NIE and TTC are sent to schools to teach subjects or levels for which they are not trained.

Problems in the follow-up of the reforms

The shortage of qualified human resources at all levels has led to a failure in establishing an adequate follow-up mechanism. Because of this, most of the reforms are without proper monitoring and evaluation, leaving the teachers to put the reforms into practice unassisted amidst the numerous difficulties facing them, as already discussed earlier. This has been recognized as a major drawback in the system and measures have been taken to rectify it.

An INSET programme has been started to carry out an impact analysis of the 'what after' of the workshops, with a team of educators being given the task of collecting and analysing data from the teachers in the schools. Another positive development is the initiation of regular curriculum reviews of different subjects. These help educators adapt to the changes.

Analysis of a Reform in the Social Studies Curriculum

Reasons for the reform

The change was brought about in the social studies curriculum from grades 6 to 10, in line with the aims and objectives of the national education policy to make the curriculum relevant to the national aspirations and in keeping with the Bhutanese culture. The old curriculum, being an imported one, was felt to be largely irrelevant to Bhutanese students.

The content lacked any input about the history, culture and geography of Bhutan, resulting in the students knowing more about other countries than about their own. The reform thus involved change in content with the inclusion of Bhutanese history and geography and also in the teaching-learning approaches with a focus on activity and inquiry-based learning.

How the reform was conducted

The social studies coordinator at CAPSS, in consultation with the Director, designed the social studies syllabus with the involvement of subject specialists from the training institutes and schoolteachers. Based on the syllabus, textbooks on the history and geography of Bhutan were developed. These went into trial use between 1988 and 1990. A review was then conducted, based on the feedback obtained from teachers. Follow-up workshops were organized for reorienting the teachers to the changes, after which the reform was implemented.

Outcomes and future prospects

While the new content was introduced into the curriculum by teachers, few changes were noticed in teaching approaches. The lecture and dictation method was still predominant with hardly any meaningful and experiential learning taking place. This may largely be due to the fact that fundamental change in teaching methods requires a change in belief about practice. To bring this about, a lot of pressure, support and guidance were needed. These elements were largely neglected due to constraints of human resources, resource materials and inadequate communication.

The social studies curriculum envisages a number of additional changes in the future. The most current issue is the integration of social studies up to grade VIII. The students will not be taught history and geography separately, instead they will learn social studies with more focus on development of values and attitudes and social skills.

Bhutanese civics will be introduced in 1999 as part of the school syllabus, so as to enable students to develop an awareness of the functioning of the government and their own civic responsibilities. Approaches to the teaching of social studies have gradually improved over the years due to the adoption of the required teaching strategies by newly trained teachers.

Maldives

The Republic of Maldives is an archipelago of approximately 1,190 coral islands located southwest of the Indian subcontinent. The islands form twenty-six natural atolls, which are grouped into twenty atolls for administrative purposes. The total population of the Maldives is around 250,000. The population is dispersed among 200 inhabited islands, with 90% of them having a population of less than 1,000. Around 25% of the population is concentrated in the capital, Male.

The system of education prevailing in the Maldives today has its roots in a traditional system of schooling that has existed for hundreds of years. These traditional schools, known as edhuruge, makthab or madhrasa, are privately owned or operated by the island communities and are usually self-financing. The edhuruge is a gathering of children in a private home with the objective of teaching them to read the Quran, to read and write Dhivehi, the mother tongue of Maldivians, and to provide some rudiments of arithmetic. The edhuruge is more formal and offers almost the same curriculum, while in the madhrasa the curriculum is more far-ranging. These schools have contributed towards achieving many educational objectives, including a high rate of literacy and the preservation of national culture and tradition (Ministry of Education, 1992). However, the present system of education is the result of a merger between the traditional system of schooling and a Western style of schooling introduced since 1960.

The Western style of schooling was introduced in English-medium schools in the capital Male as part of a conscious effort to prepare individuals for training that they would receive overseas in order to meet the increasing developmental needs of the country. Thus, the beginning of a public school system was patterned after the British system in terms of organization of curriculum and methods of instruction.

One of the most significant historical developments in education was in 1978 with the decision to unify the national education system. Under this system, schooling in the Maldives was structured on a 5-2-3-2 cycle—five years of' primary schooling leading to two years at the middle school level followed by three years of junior secondary school studies and two years of senior secondary school studies. At the end of the 3-year junior secondary cycle and the 2-year junior secondary cycle students sit the London EDEXCEL GCE Ordinary-level and Advanced-level examinations respectively.

The National Curriculum

In January 1980, the Ministry of Education (MOE) introduced the first five-year primary curriculum. In 1982, a workshop was held to review this curriculum and to produce another one for the middle-school level. The resulting revisions and re-orientation of the primary curriculum led to the introduction of the first National Curriculum (NC) in 1984.

The NC in Maldives covers the primary and middle school cycles in all subject areas. The secondary curriculum content is designed around the O-level and A-level examinations offered by EDEXCEL. However, in the case of Islamic studies, the Dhivehi language and fisheries science, the curricula are designed locally—even for the secondary levels.

Educational Goals and Objectives for Maldives

1. The goals of education follow from the national development goals. They are:

   (a) to develop capable individuals with useful occupational skills, knowledge and attitudes for national development with a sense of dignity about labour, and for preserving the nation's environmental resources.

   (b) to promote social justice and equity by ensuring universal primary education and equal educational opportunity for all citizens.

   (c) to develop, within an education system based on the principles of Islam, an awareness among all citizens that, as members of the nation, they are also part of the Muslim Ummah.

   (d) to promote in individuals a spirit of independence and self-reliance such that they may seek to enhance the quality of life by discovering ways and means of improving their own health, nutrition, and wellbeing.

   (e) to strengthen national consciousness, and to preserve the nation's cultural heritage by promoting desirable cultural values, traditions and the national language.

   (f) to provide facilities for lifelong education for all citizens, so that the individual becomes a self-learner and continues to extend his/her intellectual capacity; technical skills and ability to cope with new technologies and discoveries, and develops an appreciation and understanding of changes now occurring in the social and economic life of Maldives.

   (g) to develop a sympathetic appreciation of the diversity and interdependence of peoples in the national and international communities.

2. The major objectives 2 of education are as follows:

   (a) Expand and strengthen the provision of childhood care and education.

   (b) Provide universal basic education (grades 1-7) by the year 2000.

   (c) Increase the numbers of trained manpower.

   (d) Contribute to the national effort to increase trained manpower.

   (e) Improve educational efficiency through quality enhancement.

   (f) Improve equity in access and quality of education by gender and location.

   (g) Improve curricular relevance to prepare students both for further education and for emerging educational opportunities and to develop appropriate values and attitudes.

   (h) Improve and strengthen the management of the education system.

3. The national philosophy 3 of education includes four main aspects dealing with students' physical and emotional development, cognitive development, social and moral development and skills development. The subjects are developed so as to enhance these various aspects appropriately. Syllabuses are designed by incorporating these elements in an integrated, cohesive and well-defined manner. The teaching material or textbooks are then prepared with the aim of achieving the objectives of the syllabuses.

4. The National Curriculum 4 offers seven subjects namely: mathematics, English, Dhivehi, Islam, environmental studies, practical arts and physical education at the primary level. At middle-school level, environmental studies is replaced by social studies and general science. There are two levels of secondary education comprising a three-year programme of lower secondary education where students are prepared to take the GCE 'O'-Level examinations, and two years of upper secondary, grades 11 and 12, after which students take the GCE 'A'-Level examinations offered by EDEXCEL.

Mechanisms of Curriculum Development

The National Curriculum is based on fundamental principles within an Islamic framework. These principles, derived after several stages of consultations, encompass democracy, equity, nationalism, independence, innovation for development and strengthening of the Maldivian society. Based on these fundamental principles, the MOE, in consultation with the National Education Council (NEC), produces national objectives for the education sector.

The Educational Development Centre (EDC) is responsible for translating these national objectives into curriculum statements after appropriate consultations. Once the Minister of Education adopts the curriculum statements as policy, EDC draws up the national frameworks for individual subject areas, the syllabi, textbooks, teacher's guides and other relevant resources.

Subject panels, consisting of practising teachers and subject specialists from various sectors, including the

Department of Public Examinations and the Institute of Teacher Education, help the EDC in the process.

As of 1999, EDC is also responsible for specifying the curriculum materials for the secondary levels. The centre develops teaching materials and resources for Islamic Studies, Dhivehi and Fisheries Science. For the other subjects EDC specifies the materials and resources to be used. Even at the secondary level, subject panels assist EDC.

Problems Faced by Curriculum Developers

Curriculum developers at EDC are responsible for the formulation and development of curriculum materials. Each curriculum developer is responsible for a subject area. The curriculum developer has to design the syllabus, decide on the content and prepare textbooks and teacher's guides. In conducting these activities, curriculum developers have to overcome a number of difficulties, such as the following:

At the curriculum design level

- Some curriculum developers need further training, particularly in modern curriculum design techniques.
- There is a particular lack in the region of adequate reference materials, journals and curriculum materials used in other countries.
- There is limited access to the Internet.

At the implementation level

- There is a need for strengthening a process of regular feedback from teachers on implementation.

- There are limited opportunities for curriculum developers to observe classroom teaching.

At the evaluation level

- There is a lack of regular interaction with teachers.
- There is a lack of regular feedback from teachers.
- In some instances, teaching is not geared to achieve curriculum objectives.
- In some instances, testing and examinations are not aligned with curriculum objectives.

Curriculum Reform

Rationale for change

As local and global developments influence Maldivian society, there is recognition of the need for the syllabi and teaching materials to reflect these changes. In this respect, many emerging issues need to be incorporated into the social studies syllabus.

These include environmental issues (with special focus on the effect of greenhouse gases and the rise in sea-level), overpopulation, the challenges of living in a rapidly developing world, international understanding, tolerance, health and population education, gender prejudice and other social, economic and political issues.

Process of reform

In 1990, social studies subject-panel meetings were held to discuss the relevance, appropriateness and accuracy of the existing syllabi. Discussions generated the view that most of the topics in social studies needed to be presented in a new perspective since some of the information was outdated.

Thus, the textbooks also needed to be changed. Questionnaires were sent out to all schools that taught this subject. These questionnaires were directed at obtaining a wide range of information on the current materials. Feed- back from these schools supported the view of the panel members.

Draft syllabi for social studies were prepared under the guidance of subject experts and the subject panel. After discussions with teachers and the panel, the Ministry of Education approved the final syllabi in 1991.

The syllabi were designed to encourage changes in teaching style in order to accomplish the objectives of the National Curriculum. They encourage teachers:

- to develop metacognitive skills and understanding;
- to be problem posers and guides rather than problem solvers;
- to present the material in everyday contexts;
- to encourage wider involvement of community, parents, etc. in the learning process;
- to enhance group work; and
- to encourage process-oriented teaching.

Textbooks and teacher's guides were prepared and pretested with the help of practising teachers according to the requirements of the new syllabi. After the trials, the textbooks and teacher's guides were published.

The new syllabi and the accompanying textbooks for social studies brought very positive feedback from schools. It was claimed that students' interest in the subject had increased and that the presentation and layout of the new textbooks stimulated interest, generating lively classroom discussions. Teachers also indicated that the curriculum introduced and enhanced research skills in students, fostering their motivation to learn. It also introduced critical thinking skills, making students more active participants in class. However, some schools noted that the level of English used in the texts was higher than in other subjects, which posed some problems for stu-dents.

The Maldives islands are widely dispersed and, as access to some of them is not very frequent, curriculum developers do not receive regular feedback from schools. At the implementation stage, curriculum developers need contact with teachers to get first-hand information about the syllabuses or teaching material. To gauge the effectiveness of these materials, systematic evaluation is also of utmost importance. Measures need to be taken to ensure that teachers are informed of the evaluation results so that steps can be taken to remedy the situation.

One of the major constraints in curriculum development is the need for further streamlining of the curriculum development process. In the new framework, EDC's role will shift more towards the management of curriculum development, while increasing the involvement of experienced teachers in the process. As teachers are the deliverers of the curriculum at classroom level, effective implementation largely depends on them.

Several reforms have already been introduced into the content and teaching methodologies of the national curriculum that came into effect in 1984. However, this curriculum now needs a major revision to adjust and strengthen it to enable our citizens to face the challenges of the twenty first century. A major nationwide curriculum review activity is planned for April 1999.

Nepal

A number of high-level government documents guide the development of curricula. They include the Secondary Education Perspective Plan (1996-2011), the Secondary Education Action Plan (1997-2002) and a recent High-Level Education Commission Report (1998).

Organisational Structure and Mechanisms in Curriculum Reform

The curriculum planned at the central level is modified by all the processes leading to its adoption. In the classroom at the secondary level most institutionalized activity is centrally controlled.

Ministry of education

The task of initiating educational activities throughout Nepal lies with the Ministry of Education (MOE). The Ministry is responsible for educational planning and management, as well as in improving service delivery systems across the country. MOE is composed of three divisions: Planning; General Administration; and Educational Administration.

Educational programmes and services are prepared by: the Curriculum Development Centre;

— the Secondary Education Development Centre; the Distance Education Centre;

— the Office of the Controller of Examinations;

— the National Centre for Educational Development;

— the regional education directorates and district education offices.

From July 1999 a new structure will be implemented with the formation of a Department of Secondary, Education, containing a Primary and Basic Education Division and a Secondary and Higher Secondary Division. This will separate policy making from executive actions.

The National Curriculum Council

A high-level National Curriculum Council (NCC), chaired by the Minister of Education, approves all curricula and guides the detailed developmental work of the Curriculum Development Centre (CDC) by setting operational and administrative policy.

Technical Committees

The NCC forms ad-hoc technical committees when additional advice is required. Matters concerning the relevance of curricula drafted by CDC may be referred to such a technical committee if the NCC feels additional advice is necessary.

Curriculum Development Centre

The CDC is responsible for the maintenance,

transmission and renewal of the school-level curriculum and is also concerned with pre-primary education. (See below for further discussion of CDC).

The Secondary Leaving Certificate Board

The Secondary Leaving Certificate Board sets policies and makes decisions relating to the School-Leaving Certificate (SLC), which are then implemented by the Office of the Controller of Examinations (OCE).

A reformed SLC, with single subject certification is planned for July 2001. The courses leading to this examination are to be implemented from grade 9, beginning in July 1999.

The Secondary Education Development Centre

The Secondary Education Development Centre (SEDEC) is responsible for a range of in-service training activities at the secondary level. SEDEC operates through twenty-five secondary education development units at locations, which allow for national coverage.

The training activities also support the work of the Curriculum Development Centre and the OCE.

Janak Educational Materials Centre

The Janak Educational Materials Centre (JEMC), operating as a public limited company, produces and distributes school textbooks throughout Nepal. JEMC's Board of Directors is comprised of representatives from concerned ministries and organizations.

The Curriculum Development Centre

Responsibilities and activities

The CDC is responsible for the maintenance, transmission and renewal of the school education curriculum. The wide-ranging activities of the centre include developing, revising and disseminating textbooks and teacher's support materials.

A programme of seminars and workshops supports these activities. CDC's development and monitoring work is carried out by specialized curriculum subject units, advised by curriculum subject specialist committees. Subject units cover languages, science and maths, social studies, health and physical education.

To support CDC's activities, various studies and surveys are conducted on curriculum-related issues and problems. The activities of CDC give rise to a wide range of relationships with other institutions.

The most important of these is with the teachers and student in schools, who are the immediate end-users of the centre's products. CDC also incorporates a publishing unit.

The Publishing Unit (PU)

The PU (in collaboration with subject specialist units, their advisory subject specialist committees, subject advisers and consultants) sets textbook specifications. According to prescribed procedures, the PU also selects textbook writers on the basis of: subject knowledge, classroom experience and sample materials reviewed by teachers/ subject experts.

A PU staff member serves as the managing editor, and is responsible for briefing contracted writers and liaising closely with them to ensure quality and schedule controls, until the camera-ready copy goes to the printers.

The PU manager also arranges distribution of the draft materials to be tested in schools and validated by teacher groups. The managing editor, unit specialist, subject committee members, advisers and specialists all visit schools to collect comments which are subsequently relayed to the writers.

Subject Advisory Committees

The role of these committees is to advise on the preparation and revision of the curriculum, and the preparation, revision and evaluation of textbooks and teachers guides.

The Curriculum Officers, as members of the committees, also participate in these activities and provide the secretariat that promotes the committee's work. Subcommittees are established to carry out specialist developmental inputs. The subject committees cover Nepali, English, science, mathematics, social studies, and health, population and environment (HPE).

Task Committees

Like the publishing unit, the task committees cut across the boundaries of the various specialist units. Examples are the formative assessment committee and the dissemination committee. Task committees are formed to advise the cross-boundary projects managing officer on policy and operational matters.

Developments in the Design, Implementation and Follow-up of Curriculum Reform

Aims of secondary education

The general aims of secondary education are to: produce healthy citizens who are: familiar with the national tradition, culture, social environment, democratic values; able to use language effectively in daily life; aware of scientific issues; creative, cooperative, industrious; able to contribute to economic development.

The secondary curriculum

The lower secondary curriculum (grades 6, 7 and 8) and the secondary curriculum (grades 9 and 10) are constructed with core subjects and optional subjects. The five lower secondary core subjects are Nepali, English, math, science and social studies.

The six secondary core subjects are Nepali, English, math, science, social studies, health, population and environment (HPE).

Table 5

Secondary school curriculum structure—general secondary school level

subject	Classes 9 and 10	
	Weightage	Full Mark
1 Nepali	5	100
2 Mathematics	5	100
3 English	5	100
4 Science	5	100
5 Social studies	5	100

6 Health, Population and Environmental Education	4	100
7 Optional Paper I	5	100
8 Optional Paper II	5	100
Total	39	800

A. Option 1 paper subjects (any one)

Languages: Nepali, Arabic, Avadhi, Bhojpuri, Bengalit, Chinese, Hindi, Japanese, Maithili, Sanskrit, Tibetan, Persian, Hebrew, Urdit, English, French, German, Greek, Latin, Russian, Spanish. (Other national languages of Nepal will be included in the curriculum, provided that grammar books, teaching materials, etc., are available.)

Humanities, Social Science: history, geography, civics, economics, sociology.

Optional mathematics

B. Option 2 Paper subjects (any one)

Interdisciplinary: agricultural education, food science, architectural education, industrial education, office management and accounting, auditing, typing and shorthand, computer science, home science, handicrafts painting, sewing and knitting, bamboo-work, dance, music, Ayurveda naturpathy, health and physical education, photography, journalism, instrumentation.

Secondary Education Development Project

The Secondary Education Development Project (SEDP)

began in 1993. SEDP originally aimed at improving and reinforcing three subjects (English, science, mathematics). In 1997, support to Nepali and social studies was added. SEDP also has the goal of reforming the examination system and providing materials and equipment to selected secondary schools. The project has been providing support services through the Secondary Education Development Centre and the twenty-five training centres.

Accomplishments

As of July 1998, CDC had produced ten curriculum booklets outlining the lower secondary curriculum (grades 6-8) and the secondary curriculum (grades 9 and 10) and covering all core subjects therein. The curriculum and textbooks for grades 6 (1996), 7 (1997) and 8 have been printed and distributed (1998). The lower secondary curriculum is being prepared for publication. However, English is the only subject in which teacher's guides have so far been produced.

In July 1998, the National Curriculum Council (NCC) decided to restructure the curriculum of grades 9 and 10, to allow for the inclusion of a new sixth core subject, health, population and environment (HPE). This reduced English, Nepali, mathematics and science from six to five periods each week. The curriculum was adjusted in line with the reduction of periods. The grade 9 production schedule for textbooks and teacher's guides has now been separated from that of grade 10. The grade 9 textbooks for the six core subjects were scheduled for printing by the end of March 1999, while completion of grade 9 teacher's guides was foreseen for the end of April 1999.

CDC has formulated a seven-stage dissemination strategy for the grades 9 and 10 curriculum. The first stage (approval) was completed in November 1998. Included in the strategy are: detailed planning, package development, training of master facilitators and facilitators, training of head-teachers, cluster-based and school-based workshops. The full programme will be completed by the end of July 1999.

The Publishing Unit's first textbooks are clearly of a better quality than previous CDC/SEDP outputs. The unit has also produced a four-page CDC bulletin of a high standard (February 1998) to publicize its activities, as well as a leaflet in English and Nepali. Textbooks have been monitored for gender, socioeconomic and regional equity.

National goals of education

The National Goals of Education frame all the detailed technical work of curriculum development and should be reflected in all documents and materials developed by the Curriculum Development Centre.

The national education goals are to:

- nurture and develop the personalities and inherent talents in each person;
- instill respect for human values and the will to safeguard national and social beliefs so as to help develop a healthy social unity;
- help the individual to socialize, enhancing social unity;
- help the individual keep his or her identity in the national and international context and to help him/

her lead a socially harmonious life in the modern world;

- assist the modernization of the country by creating able manpower for its development;
- teach the thoughtful protection and wise use of Nepal's natural resources;
- bring those who are underprivileged into the mainstream of the nation.

Developments and Challenges in the Design, Implementation and follow-up of Curriculum Reform

While the capacity of CDC to handle complex tasks is clearly improving, the capacity to plan and to develop human resources has certain constraints due to the rate of staff changeovers. This makes the institutionalization of curriculum development design processes very difficult. These staff changes are at all professional and administrative levels of the organization.

The same changes create problems of continuity and liaison with other organizations connected with the implementation process. These institutions 'District Education Offices, Regional Education Offices, OCE and SEDEC—also have high staff instability.

There are very few formalized follow-up activities, except by the SEDP BME Unit. These are mainly concerned with project evaluation.

Reforming the Curriculum with special emphasis on social studies

As described earlier all core curricula and many optional subjects have been changed in recent years. In the development of all core curricula there has been tension between traditionalists and modernists, as well as between nationalists and those in favour of globalisation or wider horizons—those who speak for 'our values' and those who speak of 'global values'.

Balancing these diverse views is a problem for all curriculum developers. No curriculum subject can avoid these controversies. While in science and mathematics the debate is narrower, in English and Nepali there are different dimensions due to the source of each individual language. Both of the two newer subjects—social studies and HPE—have proved to be controversial in different ways.

Translating the goals, general objectives and specific objectives of the social studies curriculum into a useful textbook proved difficult. Although there are many dimensions to the discussion, the fundamental debate concerns whether education is about passing knowledge or learning skills—or what is the balance between the two. Members of the subject committee did not always agree with those who set the framework for developing the new textbook, creating what is hopefully a creative tension.

Those setting the framework for developing the new textbook felt that the following factors are all important in the writing of a new style textbook:

- Each chapter should have clearly thought-out learning outcomes. These will include not only factual information for knowledge and understanding, but specific skills such as interpreting a bar chart, locating places of historical importance, presenting an argument in favour of a certain course of action and collecting local data.

- The earlier textbooks mostly contained only factual information, followed by recall questions. The new textbook must present information in different forms (text, statistics, pictures, photographs, diagrams, graphs and charts, maps, newspaper items, source documents) and provide challenging questions to help students understand, interpret, analyse and evaluate the information.
- The textbook must include many project-related activities, starting with simple tasks, and moving towards longer projects. This will mean that most of the work studied has a local component and thus is of genuine relevance to the students. It will also mean that students can experience research activities, gaining practical investigation and analytical skills, and learning to present their findings. It will also help them to work together cooperatively.
- The students should be able to see what skills they are learning in each chapter and gain a sense of achievement and progress towards the school-leaving certificate (SLC). This may be done with a summary of chapters or topics. The exercises given in the textbook will not only test knowledge and understanding, but will expect analysis and evaluation of the information, and well-thought-out answers. They will also need to encourage the practice of practical skills and abilities. This will provide practice for new SLC-type questions.

Social studies curriculum

Objectives

There are twenty-eight general objectives listed in the grades 9 and 10 social studies curricula. Highly specific objectives are listed for grade 9 (twenty-seven objectives) and grade 10 (twenty-nine objectives).

Abilities

On achieving the course objectives, students will be able to demonstrate a wide range of abilities. Some examples of the abilities associated with knowledge and understanding and practical abilities are as follows:

Ability 1: Knowledge and understanding.

1. Describing projects in different zones and development regions;
2. Describing achievements of Nepal in fields of education, health, transportation, telecommunications, electricity and water supply;
3. Discussing the role of skilled manpower in the development of the infrastructure of Nepal;
4. Stating the role of international organizations in solving social problems;
5. Explaining different climates and the elements that affect them;
6. Giving a short introduction to the geo-economic activities of continents;
7. Identifying the problems created by population growth and migration and finding out ways to participate in solving them;

8. Describing the physical features of the Earth;
9. Examining the impact of landslides on the physical features of Nepal and participating in the task of avoiding them;
10. Listing the agricultural products grown in the various geographical areas.

Ability 2: Practical abilities.

1. Maintaining national dignity;
2. Drawing a map of Nepal and filling in the main industrial centres and roads;
3. Demonstrating models in class;
4. Analysing the data presented in charts;
5. Locating historical sites on a map;
6. Investigating the problems of population growth;
7. Appreciating the contributions of our national heroes;
8. Applying the knowledge of social studies for the good of society;
9. Drawing a picture of the Himalayan region;
10. Recording the maximum rainfall of the month;
11. Designing a research proposal to find out about social evils.

Criteria

The new-style social studies textbook must be developed so that students can be thoroughly prepared to take the new SLC examination. The textbook must help them not only to understand the content of the course, but also to develop the necessary skills and ability to think critically about the different topics. Thus, each chapter should have clearly thought-out learning outcomes. These will include not only factual information for knowledge and understanding, but will also include specific skills such as those outlined in the previous section. After studying this lesson the student will be able to:

- interpret a bar chart;
- locate places of historical importance;
- present an argument in favour of a certain course of action;
- collect local data.

The earlier textbooks contained only factual information, followed by recall questions. To prepare for the new SLC examination, the new textbooks must present information in different forms (text, statistics, pictures, photographs, diagrams, graphs and charts, maps, newspaper items, source documents) and provide challenging questions to help students understand, interpret, analyse and evaluate the information.

As 30% of the new SLC marks will be given for project-style work to be carried out during the year, the textbook must include many such activities; starting with simple tasks, and evolving to longer projects. This will mean that most of the material studied has a local component and thus is of relevance to the students. It will also mean that students can undertake genuine research, and gain practical skills in investigating, analysing and presentating their findings. It will also help them to work together cooperatively in groups. Such tasks are illustrated below.

Examples

- draw up a plan of your VDC, mark the water;
- prepare a poster or a talk to stop young people from experimenting with drugs;
- survey the type and number of animals kept in the local community;
- write and perform a short historical drama;
- keep a record of local weather over a long period and prepare a suitable display, such as a bar chart or graph.

The students should be able to see what skills they are learning in each chapter and gain a sense of achievement and progress towards the SLC. The exercises given in the textbook will not only test knowledge and understanding, but will require analysis and evaluation of the information and well thought-out answers. They will also need to encourage the practice of practical skills and abilities. This will provide practice for new SLC type questions.

Pakistan

Education in Pakistan is essentially a provincial affair. However, education is considered to be a vital source of nation-building. Therefore, in order to ensure national cohesion, integration and preservation of the ideological foundation of the State, certain educational functions are the responsibilities of the Federation—via the Federal Ministry of Education. These responsibilities include:

1. curriculum,
2. syllabus,

3. planning,
4. policy,and
5. educational standards.

The 1976 Act of Parliament authorized the Ministry of Education (MOE) to appoint competent authorities to perform the following curriculum-related functions:

— In connection with the implementation of the education policy of the Federal Government of Pakistan (GOP), prepare or commission: schemes for studies; curricula, textbook manuscripts and strategic schedules for their introduction in various classes of educational institutions;

— Approve manuscripts of textbooks produced by other agencies, before they are prescribed in various classes of an educational institution;

— Direct any person or agency in writing to delete, amend or withdraw any portion, or the whole, of a curriculum, textbook or reference material prescribed for any class of an educational institution.

Accordingly, a Central/National Bureau of Curriculum and Textbooks (NBCT, commonly known as the Curriculum Wing) was appointed to supervise curriculum and textbooks development/approval and to maintain curriculum standards from the primary through to the higher secondary levels.

As a logical sequence to this action, four counterpart provincial curriculum centres (one in each province) were established to ensure provincial collaboration and evolve consensus in all activities falling within the purview of the Federation. This initiative was followed by the establishment of four Provincial Textbook Boards (PTTB)–one in each province.

Within their respective jurisdictions, these PTTBs are responsible for preparing, publishing, stocking, distributing and marketing school textbooks Boards of Intermediate and Secondary Education responsible for conduct of examinations at Secondary (IX-X) and Higher Secondary (XI-XII) levels were also established at each of the divisional headquarters.

Subsequently, another institution was established—the Inter-Board Committee of Chairmen (IBCC)—with the following objectives:

— To exchange information among the member boards on all aspects of secondary and higher secondary education;

— To achieve a fair measure of uniformity in academic evaluation standards;

— To promote inter-board curricular and extracurricular activities;

— To serve as a board chief executives' discussion and consultation forum for all matters relating to secondary and higher secondary education development, and making suitable recommendations to the GOP;

— Advise on and facilitate the exchange of teachers and students;

— Perform such other functions as may be incidental or conducive to the attainment of the above objectives.

Curriculum Development Process

Reform

It may be noted that the process of curriculum reform in Pakistan has been introduced as part of the successive series of national education policies.

The following six-phase strategy has been adopted for implementing curriculum change:

1. Evolution of curriculum objectives (by level);
2. Development of scheme of studies (by level);
3. Development of syllabus of each subjects;
4. Development of textbooks/instructional materials;
5. Review/approval of textual material;
6. Teacher training.

Table 6
Education policy and curriculum reform cycle

National Education Policy	Curriculum reform cylce
1972	Ist cylce, 1973-76
1979	2nd cylce, 1982-85
1992	3rd cylce, 1992-95
1998	4th cylce, 1998-01

Developing objectives

Curriculum objectives are basically derived from the recommendations of National Education Policy, national level seminars and other forums (e.g. forums of the Inter-Board Committee of Chairmen (IBCC) and research studies conducted at provincial curriculum centres). The NBCT prepares the draft of objectives; which are widely circulated among the provincial institutions responsible for curriculum development, teacher training and examination.

Based on their views/comments, these objectives are finalized. They are subsequently translated into the specific teaching objectives for various subjects. Several factors are considered in finalizing curriculum objectives; including the requirements that objectives should:

(a) be precise;

(b) assist in the selection of teaching strategy;

(c) produce a designated behaviour pattern;

(d) enable the teachers to measure or evaluate the quality and effectiveness of learning.

The studies scheme

The scheme of studies is based on three key factors:

(1) the national education policy;

(2) market demand;

(3) global issues that relate to new or contemporary education dimensions.

Task work in this area is undertaken with active participation of the provincial government, research organizations and experts; as well as feedback from the IBCC.

Development of syllabi

Based on the objectives and scheme of studies, subject specific syllabi are prepared in consultation with: provincial curriculum centres; subject experts; and psychologists and serving teachers.

Collectively, they ensure that the syllabi, in all respects, satisfy the following conditions:

1. They are based on the needs of the learner/child;
2. They take into account the existing knowledge and environmental experience of the learner;
3. The developmental level of the learner is considered in the cognitive, effectiveness and psycho-motor domains;
4. The contents should be focused on attaining the objective(s).

Textbook development

Provincial Textbook Boards (PTBB) are responsible for development of textbooks according to the approved syllabi. Established lists of textbook writers in various subjects are kept. From these lists, invitations are issued to writers to submit draft materials within the prescribed syllabus parameters.

Selections are made on the basis of the quality and relevance of materials submitted to local situations. Finally, the selected materials are transformed into textbooks; the final versions of which are sent to the NBCT for approval.

Review and approval

A National Review Committee, comprising five or six members includes: at least one expert from the Syllabus Formulation Committee; two subject experts; two schoolteachers (one teaching the relevant material and one from a teacher-training institute).

On receipt of textual materials from PTBB, this committee conducts textbook reviews based on the following parameters:

(a) the book truly reflects the curriculum;

(b) it meets the objectives stated in the curriculum;

(c) the book does not contain any material repugnant to Islamic and Pakistani ideology.

In the case of approval, the textbook is sent back for publishing and distribution. In case of objection, the specific complaints are relayed along wiih revision recommendations.

Teacher training

Teacher training for curriculum implementation is the exclusive responsibility of the provincial government. However, it is now being stressed that each textbook must have a teacher's guide also approved by the NBCT. In some cases, assistance in the training of master trainers is provided to provincial governments.

Curriculum Development Pitfalls

Several major obstacles affecting the quality and effectiveness of the curriculum development process in Pakistan are summarized below.

Expertise

Some serving teachers are, of course, involved in curriculum development. But notwithstanding their outstanding subject area expertise, their contribution to the curriculum development is, for all practical purposes, nominal. The main reason for this is that they lack the requisite expertise.

The existing training programmes provide little exposure in this area, and the teachers—academic qualifications do not necessarily contribute to curricular creativity. Therefore, at best, the teachers are able to provide opinions about the compatibility between specific concepts or content and the intellectual development level of the children in a specific age group or grade.

However, this guidance often reflects, in part, a particular situation with which the teachers have been dealing (e.g. children from a rural background) and, in part, their own capability to render a specific concept comprehensible.

Textbook quality

Textbooks often do not reflect the curriculum. Of course, it requires considerable experience and skill to: translate the curriculum in a style that covers the objectives; simultaneously take into consideration the children's language proficiency and background knowledge; and concurrently arrange the content in a logical sequence in a stimulating manner. But the all-important self-assessment questions or activities are invariably missing.

Implementation and follow-up

The third problem is that there is lack of follow-up of actual curriculum implementation in classroom practice. The curriculum actually implemented is generally different from the official curriculum document. The classroom teacher, who primarily focuses on the textbooks and assessment, does not take into account the educational objectives. No evaluation of the implemented curriculum is carried out; hence no feedback is received to revise the curriculum. In short, each of the steps in the curriculum development process, as outlined above, tends to occur in isolation from the others and there is no visible coherent curriculum development activity.

Sri Lanka

In Sri Lanka, the Ministry of Education and the National Education Commission are responsible for all curriculum-related policy making. However, the National Institute of Education (NIE) has the overall responsibility for curriculum design and development, preparation of syllabi, teacher's guides and textbooks.

A council empowered to take all policy and high-level administrative decisions on matters coming under its purview governs the NIE: Its staff consists of curriculum teams of specialist officers and is augmented by teacher educators and teachers seconded for service to the respective teams. Consultation takes place during the curriculum development process and subsequent implementation, with subject specialists and professionals outside of NIE, as well as affected parties.

Educational Goals

Sri Lanka's educational goals can be summarized as follows:

— To develop and understand the cultural and religious heritage and the democratic traditions of the country, as well as an appreciation of the contributions made by the different ethnic groups to the national culture;

— To develop a basic understanding of the environment and skills relevant to the needs of life and society;

— To cultivate an appreciation of the arts, literature and science;

— To develop attitudes conducive to harmonious relations among the different ethnic groups;

— To promote moral, spiritual and physical development;

— To inculcate a sense of commitment to national development;

— To develop and promote a system for the acquisition of technical knowledge and vocational skills to meet the manpower needs of the country;

— To promote lifelong education and knowledge renewal through programmes of formal and non-formal education;

— To promote the democratization of education.

Pre-reform Education System and Curriculum

Prior to the education reform initiatives in Sri Lanka, the formal pre-tertiary education system consisted of four stages:

1. primary: grades 1-5;
2. junior secondary: grades 6-8;
3. senior secondary: grades 9-11;
4. collegiate: grades 12-13.

There was a commonly prescribed curriculum for grades 1 to 11.

The lower primary stage was characterized by a highly integrated curriculum (first language, mathematics, environmental studies, creative-aesthetic activities, and religion). In the upper primary stage, the curriculum was semi-integrated, with more emphasis on subject competencies. At this level, a beginning science course and English as a second language were introduced.

At the secondary stage, the curriculum consisted of the following subjects, some of which were interdisciplinary in nature: religion, first language, English, mathematics, integrated science, social studies, and history, aesthetic education and a life-skills/technical subject.

At the end of grade 11 (which is also the end of general education) the General Certificate of Education Ordinary Level (GCE-O-Level) examination is administered.

Educational reform

A new structure for primary education

The Sri Lankan education system is now in the process of being restructured and a number of curriculum reforms are planned or are already underway. A new primary level structure intended to be more suitable to the proposed curriculum reform is being implemented. As a result of this change, grades 1-5 will constitute a primary stage segment. Under this framework, the primary cycle is divided into three key stages (KS):

— KS-1, grades 1 and 2;

— KS-2, grades 3 and 4; and

— KS-3, grade 5.

Objectives of the reform

The new, reformed primary education programme objectives listed below have evolved from the larger framework of national education goals, namely:

— development of a child-centred curriculum;

— development of essential as well as desirable competencies during the key stages;

— training of primary grade teachers to implement the revised curriculum;

— provision of adequate facilities and materials to all primary schools;

— establishment of an equal opportunity network throughout the country.

The new curriculum

The reforms will see the countrywide introduction of a highly integrated curriculum at the lower primary stage, with the subject-area environment-related activities, which encompasses several disciplines. Another notable modification related to integration of content is the introduction of activity-based oral English in KS-1. The objective is to create a classroom environment where children and teachers use a mix of mother tongue and conversational English.

Appropriate vocabulary will be developed through activity learning and games. Additionally, there is a provision for co-curricular work in all the key stages. The number of subject areas in the curriculum is now being limited to four:

1) languages;
2) mathematics;
3) religion; and
4) environment-related activities.

In the languages component, the formal teaching of English, beginning with KS-2, is being introduced; as well as a second national language (Sinhala/Tamil)-from KS-3. In the past, even at primary level, the content of subjects received the greatest emphasis. However, nowadays the focus will be placed on competencies that children are expected to have acquired at the end of their general education.

This new curriculum establishes a comprehensive set of basic competencies in communications, ethics and religion, environment, learning, enjoyment and leisure. Entry competencies will also be identified, using specially designed assessment instruments, enabling the grade 1 teacher to cater more effectively to children's individual needs. Furthermore, the essential competencies that children are expected to have mastered at the end of each key stage will be identified and this information made available to teachers.

Table 7

New primary stage competencies

Communications: comprises three subsets: literacy (listening attentively; speaking clearly; reading with understanding; writing accurately and lucidly); numeracy (using numbers: counting, calculating, measuring systematically); graphics (making sense of line, form; expressing and recording details, instructions, ideas, with line, form and colour).

Environment: comprises three parts: social (social awareness and relationships, personal conduct, rights, responsibilities, duties and obligations); biological (awareness, sensitivity and skills linked to the living world, man and the ecosystem.); physical (awareness, sensitivity and skills relating to space, energy, fuels, matter, materials and their links with human life. Also included are the skills in using tools to shape and form materials for living and learning).

Ethics and religion: comprises values and attitudes deemed essential for individuals to assimilate, so that they may function in a manner consistent with the ethical, moral and religious modes of conduct.

Play and leisure: related to human emotions that find expression in play, sports and various leisure pursuits essential for mental and physical well-being. They are also connected with such values as: co-operation, team work, healthy life and work competition. Also included are aesthetic and creative activities. Learning to learn: related to human needs in a rapidly changing, complex, crowded world where learning will require constant review and updating. Includes developing skills of awareness, attentiveness, and perseverance.

The information revolution has rendered this competency essential.

Teachers will be encouraged to ensure that at the end of each KS, almost all children in their class have reached the mastery level in the essential competencies, with special emphasis on first language and mathematics. In this context, the practice will be to assign the same class teacher for KS 1 and KS 2.

The new teaching/learning methodology will incorporate an appropriate mix of play, activity and deskwork, the proportion of each component varying gradually with successive grades. The new curriculum also incorporates cross-age play and activity opportunities, where KS-1 children interact with children from grade 6.

There will be continuous classroom-based assessment, with increased emphasis on the use of informal methods. This represents an attempt to deviate from past assessment techniques (which encourage comparative student achievement) and move towards criterion-referenced assessment techniques. Entry competency tests for grade 1 and terminal competency tests at the end of each key stage will be developed.

The remaining tasks to be carried out include: preparation of a classroom-based evaluation framework; development of training material; and the training of teachers and supervisors. A booklet will be produced on improving testing techniques. Also, a research committee will be set up to carry out action research, surveys and evaluation on special areas, such as group work, multi-grade, multi-level teaching, gifted children and on-going aspects of the curriculum development process, including teacher training.

Resource materials

A steering committee will decide on the content and layout of textbooks and select the panel of writers who will be registered with the National Institute of Education

(NIE). Books will be reviewed by a panel and approved by the steering committee prior to publication. Additional resource materials for primary classes will be prepared at the level of the school, the resource centre and the province with NIE assistance. The Education Publication Department (MOE) and NIE are collectively responsible for printing and distributing teaching and resource materials.

Implementation schedule

The new primary curriculum was introduced in 1998 as a pilot project in grade 1 of Gampaha district, and introduced to the whole country during 1999. It will be progressively implemented at each grade level, terminating in grade 5 by 2003.

Teacher education

A profile of the primary school-teacher will be developed based on the vision of the primary school for the twenty-first century. Essential teacher competencies and attitudes will be identified and a new pre-service teacher education curriculum and training materials developed. The staff of colleges of education and other teacher-training institutes will undergo orientation programmes. Each training college will adopt a problem-solving school in its catchment area in order to conduct field-based activities. In-service training of primary teachers will be an integral part of the reform. The Master Teacher Programme will be strengthened.

School managers

As the primary section forms a part of the main school in

Sri Lanka, an assistant principal or a senior teacher will be entrusted with responsibility for the primary section of the main school. In schools where there is a large number of pupils, additional adequate supervisory assistance will be provided (i.e. sectional or grade co-ordinators).

Anticipated school-level management tasks include: establishing a primary education development committee; strengthening parent/community relations; formalizing collaboration with neighbouring schools through the formation of school families; developing and implementing an internal supervisory mechanism for teacher self-evaluation, as well as collegial peer evaluation.

Provincial administration

The provincial administrative structure will also be strengthened, with a separate primary education division in the Provincial Department (PPEU) being established under a senior officer. The appointment of officers responsible for primary education at the zonal level operating under the PPEU is also foreseen, as well as the creation of primary education development committees in both provinces and zones, comprised of principals, teachers, parents and community leaders.

Public awareness

This will be carried out through a mass media publicity programme involving newspapers, radio and TV and targeting school staff, parents, influential youth groups as well as the general public.

Future Prospects for Curiculum Reform

Junior secondary stage

In the near future it is projected that grades 6-9 will constitute the junior secondary stage of education, thereby functioning as the upper section of the junior school. Grade 6 will become the bridging year between the integrated curriculum of primary school and the subject based curriculum of secondary school. It will serve to inculcate the necessary study skills for secondary education while reinforcing the essential competencies to be acquired during the primary cycle, particularly in language and mathematics. The syllabi in grade 6 will be revised to meet these requirements.

There will be a common curriculum at this stage, comprising 9 subjects: first language, English, mathematics, science and technology, social studies, life skills, religion, aesthetics, health and physical education.

At the end of grade 9, a school-based examination, the Junior School Proficiency Examination, will test pupil achievement and result in the issue of a certificate. Teaching methodology will emphasize learning through projects and practical work, as spelt out in the section on practical skills education. Concepts on peace education, conflict resolution, democratic values, human rights and environmental conservation will be integrated into social studies and other relevant subject content.

Implementation plan

The revision of syllabi and course guides, training of teachers and provision of facilities were scheduled to be for completion at grade 6 level in 1998 and for implementation in January 1999. Reforms will be progressively introduced to grades 7 and 8 with the grade 9 curriculum revised in line with the new GCE-O-level curriculum.

Senior secondary stage

The present curriculum at this level is oriented to the GCE (OL or AL) examinations. The programme covers a period of 3 years; namely grades 9,10,11 for GCE (OL) and 2 years for GCE (AL) Collegiate level grades 12-13. At present, the GCE (OL) compulsory curriculum consists of the following subjects (some of which are inter disciplinary in nature): religion, first language, English, mathematics, integrated science, social studies and history, aesthetic education and life skills/technical subjects. In grade 9, students select 1 vocational type course (out of 53 such courses). In grades 10-11, 1 technical subject may be chosen from several options.

Under the proposed revisions, the time period for senior secondary education will be reduced to 2 years with classes designated grades 10 and 11. The curriculum will be made more flexible with the introduction of a number of core subjects and a number of optional subjects. Core subjects will be: religion, first language, English, mathematics, science and technology, social studies and history, aesthetic studies. Students will be permitted to select up to 3 optional subjects from the following: Sinhala/Tamil as a second language, history, geography, health and physical education, literature (Sinhala/Tamil/ English), modern or classical languages, technical subjects (from the list of approved technical subjects).

Under the reform, grade 11 remains the end of the general education for all stages. Students sit for the

General Certificate of Education Ordinary Level (GCE-OL) examination, which is a centrally planned, national school leaving examination. Only those students who achieve certain prescribed GCE-OL standards are permitted to enter the collegiate stage (about 25-30% of students).

Improving English language teaching in Sri Lanka

A special effort is being made to improve English language skills as it is realized that a better knowledge of English will improve employment opportunities and facilitate communication with the outside world. The English language teaching programme will be upgraded to provide opportunities for pupils island-wide to have equal access to English learning for comprehension and communication. Teachers of English will be provided with opportunities and incentives to improve their proficiency in English and skills in teaching English.

7

Challenges of Educational Technology

Following are the 10 challenges of educational technology:

1. We need more effective models of learning programs that balance the "virtual and the visceral" - effectively combining on-screen activities with hands-on construction kits, design challenges, probeware, discovery labs, and real world explorations.
2. We need better Web-based multimedia reference sites for learning with simple interfaces and search engines, interactive simulations, comprehensive and updated guides to related Web sites, and simple tools for learners and experts to contribute their ideas and comments to the knowledge base.
3. We need a wealth of high-quality, instructional and constructional learning simulations and tools for the creation of simulations of all kinds, from games and scenario-based simulations to virtual construction kits and virtual simulators of complex environments and processes.

4. We need a quantum leap in ease of use and useful results in information searching, organizing and reporting tools, especially for the Web, and for databases of content knowledge and learning activities.

5. We need to make the entire database development, sharing, and maintenance process much simpler so that we can more easily create useful online knowledge bases; dynamic, database-driven Web sites; personal learning history databases with multimedia portfolios of work; and large-scale education information systems that help us track Knowledge Age educational performance.

6. We need much better online collaboration and communication tools so that online discussions, live presentations with audience questions, groupwork, surveying and polling, and getting help online can actually be fun.

7. We need online learning assessment systems based on both the 3 Rs and the 7 Cs that combine simulations, concept mapping, reflective essay questions, portfolio presentations and the reporting of results from performance-based tasks. We also need a system to make it easy for content and learning experts to help review and comment on these portfolios and performance tasks.

8. We need more places for designing and constructing "gizmos, gadgets, and useful things" - workshops, labs, "garages," etc. - with real tools, construction materials, bins of parts, safe places to put things together and take things apart, and with access to online construction tips and exhibits of other students' inventions and experiments. This sort of

constructive "tinkering," so valuable to learning, is fast becoming an endangered species in our ecology of educational experiences.

9. We need to apply all of our educational technology talent to the challenge of preparing teachers, parents and other helpers and learning guides to effectively integrate the use of all kinds of technologies, from hand lenses to supercomputers, into the everyday experiences of all learners.

10. We need to go outside, breathe deep, take a walk, smell the flowers, and forget about technology at least once a day.

We have seen some of the important work that must be done for technology to continue being an effective catalyst for learning and education reform. These are just a few of the needed pieces in a complex, 3-D educational jigsaw puzzle of social, political, economic, infrastructural and, most important, human components. The challenges that the Knowledge Age brings to learning and education are great, but the promise of a new Renaissance of learning and knowledge in our society is even greater. There is much good work to be done in helping to make this promise a reality for all lifelong learners and workers in our new Knowledge Age.

Information technology in schools validate that new technology-based models of teaching and learning have the power to dramatically improve educational outcomes. As a result, many people are asking how to scale-up the scattered, successful "islands of innovation" instructional technology has empowered into universal improvements in schooling enabled by major shifts in standard educational practices. Undertaking "systemic reform" (sustained, large-scale, simultaneous innovation in curriculum; pedagogy; assessment; professional development; administration; incentives; and partnerships for learning among schools, businesses, homes, and community settings) requires policies and practices different than fostering pilot projects for small-scale educational improvement.

Systemic reform involves moving from utilizing special, external resources to reconfiguring existing budgets in order to free up money for innovation. Without undercutting their power, change strategies effective when pioneered by leaders in educational innovation must be modified to be implemented by typical educators. Technology-based innovations offer special challenges and opportunities in this scaling-up process.

Systemic reform is not possible without utilizing the full power of high performance computing and communications to enhance the reshaping of schools. Yet the cost of technology, its rapid evolution, and the special knowledge and skills required of its users pose substantial barriers to effective utilization.

Giving all students continuous access to multimedia-capable, Internet-connected computers is currently quite fashionable. For politicians, the Internet in every classroom has become the modern equivalent of the promised "chicken in every pot." Information technology vendors are offering special programs to encourage massive educational purchases. States are setting aside substantial amounts of money for building information infrastructures dedicated to instructional usage.

Multimedia-capable, Internet-connected computers are seen by many as magical devices, "silver bullets" to solve the problems of schools. Teachers and administrators who use new media are assumed to be automatically more effective than those who do not. Classroom computers are envisioned as a technology comparable to fire: just by sitting near these devices, students get a benefit from them, as knowledge and skills radiate from the monitors into their minds.

Classroom computers that are acquired as panaceas end up as doorstops. Information technology is a cost-effective investment only in the context of systemic reform. Unless other simultaneous innovations in pedagogy, curriculum, assessment, and school organization are coupled to the usage of instructional technology, the time and effort expended on implementing these devices produces few improvements in educational outcomes-and reinforces many educators' cynicism about fads based on magical machines.

Computers are envisioned as ways to empower "teaching by telling" and "learning by listening," serving as a fire hose to spray information from the Internet into learners' minds. However, even without educational technology, classrooms are already drowning in data, and an overcrowded curriculum puts students and teachers on the brink of intellectual indigestion. Adding additional information, even when coated with multimedia bells-and-whistles, is likely to worsen rather than improve educational settings.

Professional.development needs are more complex than increasing educators' technical literacy. The issue is building teachers' knowledge and skills in alternative types of pedagogy and content, and such an increase in human capabilities requires substantial funding that will be unavailable if almost all resources are put into hardware. Third, the continuing costs of maintaining and upgrading a massive infusion of school-based technology would be prohibitive.

High performance computing and communications requires high tech skills to keep operational and will become obsolete in five to seven years as information technology continues its rapid advance. Yet taxpayers now see computers as similar to blackboards: buy them once, and they are inexpensively in place for the lifetime of the school. School boards rapidly become restive at sizable yearly expenditures for technology maintenance and telecommunications usage-especially if, several months after installation, standardized test scores have not yet dramatically risen-and will become apoplectic if another $50B to replace obsolete equipment is required only a few years after an initial huge expenditure. For all these reasons, investing a huge sum in information infrastructures for schools is impractical and invites a later backlash against educational technology as yet another failed fad.

Students would arrive at school already imbued with some background and motivation, ripe for guided inquiry, ready for interpretation and collaborative construction of knowledge. People are spending lots of money on devices purchased for entertainment and information services: televisions, videotape players, computers, Web TV, videogames. What if these devices-many ubiquitous in rich and poor homes, urban and rural areas-were also utilized for educational purposes, even though not acquired for that reason? By off-loading from classroom settings some of the burden of presenting material and inducing motivation, learning activities that use the technology infrastructure outside of schools would reduce the amount of money needed for adequate levels of classroom-based technology.

Such a strategy also enables teachers to focus on students' interpretation and expressive articulation without feeling obligated to use technology in every step of the process. Such a model of "distributed learning" involves orchestrating educational activities among classrooms, workplaces, homes, and community settings. This pedagogical strategy models for students that learning is integral to all aspects of life-not just schooling-and that people adept at learning are fluent in using many types of information tools scattered throughout the everyday context.

Such an educational approach also can build partnerships for learning between teachers and families; this is important because parental involvement is certainly one of the most powerful levers in increasing any student's educational performance. In other words, unless "systemic reform" in education is conducted with one boundary of the system around the school and another boundary around the society, its affordability and sustainability are doubtful. As a bridge across these boundaries, new media can play a vital role in facilitating this bi-level approach to large-scale educational innovation.

Districts can leverage their scarce resources for innovation, as well as implement more effective educational models, by utilizing information devices outside of classrooms to create learning environments that complement computers and communications in schools. To instead saturate schools with information technology is both very expensive and less educationally effective.

Educational improvement based on distributed learning-utilizing information technologies external to school settings to enable increased interpretive and expressive activities in classrooms-does not mean that schools won't need substantial amounts of computers and communications. To empower project-based learning through guided inquiry, students must have access to sophisticated information devices in schools. Even if this is accomplished via notebook computers and wireless networks moved from class to class as required, with pupils also spending significant amounts of time learning without the aid of technology, districts must allocate more money to purchasing, maintaining, and upgrading computers and telecommunications than has been true historically.

Where will educators find the funds for equipment, software, technical staff, ongoing telecommunications services, professional development-the myriad of costs associated with a sophisticated information infrastructure? In the past, this money has come largely from special external sources: grants, community donations, bond initiatives. To be sustainable over the long run, however, resources for technology must come from reallocating existing budgets by reducing other types of expenditures. Of course, such shifts in financing are resisted by those groups whose resources are cut, and district administrators and school boards have been reluctant to take on the political challenges of changing how money is spent.

An easy way to kill educational innovations is to declare that of course they will be implemented-as long as no existing activities must be curtailed to fund new approaches. Educational organizations are unique, however, in demanding that technology implementation accomplished via add-on funding. Every other type of societal institution (e.g., factories, hospitals, retail outlets, banks) recognizes that the power of information devices stems in part from their ability to reconfigure employee roles and organizational functioning.

These establishments use the power of technology to alter their standard practices, so that the cost of computers and communications is funded by improvements in effectiveness within the organization, by doing more with less. Educators are inundated with large amounts of recordkeeping functions, and one of the most debilitating aspects of this work is the continuous reentry of identical information on different forms. Businesses have saved substantial amounts of money by altering routine information processes so that data is only entered once, then automatically flows across the entire organization to each place in which it is needed. Were educators to adopt these already proven models for cost-efficient information management, the amount of time and staff required for data entry functions would decrease markedly, freeing funding for instruction-related uses of technology.

On fundamental level, teaching is more efficient and effective with new types of technology-based curriculum and pedagogy. At present, substantial re-teaching of.knowledge and skills is required; presentational material flows into students' minds, is retained just long enough to perform on a test, and then is forgotten. Class sizes are typically between twenty-five and forty-somewhat too large for effective project-based learning, yet small given that lectures work as well for several hundred students as for several dozen. The scheduling of class periods is too short, limiting teachers and students to fragmentary presentational and practice activities.

Teachers all have comparable roles with similar pay structures-unlike other societal organizations, which have complementary staff roles with a mix of skill levels and salaries. Studies of innovation in other types of institutions indicate that successful change is always bottom-up, middle-out, and top-down. The driver for bottom-up innovation in a district is the children. Typically, students are joyful and committed when they are given the opportunity to learn by doing, to engage in collaborative construction of knowledge, and to experience mentoring relationships.

That these types of instruction are accomplished via educational technology will excite some kids, while others will be indifferent-but all will appreciate the opportunity to move beyond learning by listening. Educators can draw enormous strength and purpose from watching the eager response of their students to classroom situations that use alternative forms of pedagogy.

Often, teachers have shifted from pioneers to settlers.because they were worn down by the unceasing grind of motivating students to master uninteresting, fragmented topics; and administrators have undergone a similar loss of enthusiasm by being inundated with paperwork rather than serving as instructional coordinators. The professional commitment that kids' enthusiasm can re-inspire is a powerful driver of bottom-up change.

Many teachers entered the profession because they love students of a certain age and want to help them grow-or love their subject matter and want to share its beauty and richness. Often, these teachers feel alienated because the straightjacket of traditional instruction and school organization walls them away from meaningful relationships with their students and their subject. Similarly, many administrators want to serve as leaders and facilitators, but are forced by conventional managerial practices into being bureaucrats and bosses.

Middle-out change is empowered when educators who have given up hope of achieving their professional dreams see pioneer colleagues using technology to succeed in those goals-and realize that, if everyone made a similar commitment, no one would have to make continuous personal sacrifices to achieve this vision. The lever for top-down innovation is the community served by the district. Educators want respect-yet teaching has fallen from a revered professions to a much lower status.

The relationship between educators and their community is seldom seen as a partnership; instead, teachers and administrators often feel isolated, forced to perform a difficult task with inadequate resources. Parents, the business sector, and taxpayers bitterly debate the purpose of schools and sometimes attempt to micro-manage their operation. In contrast, when homes, classrooms, workplaces and community settings are linked via new media to achieve distributed learning, much more positive interactions emerge between schools and society.

Educators can move from isolation to collaboration with the community, from a position of low esteem to an respected role in orchestrating children's learning across a spectrum of settings. This shift in status is a powerful driver for innovation. To activate these bottom-up, middle-out, and top-down forces for improvement, educators must take the lead in developing a shared vision for systemic reform, distributed learning, and sophisticated utilization of technology.

Making such a commitment to large-scale educational innovation is not only the right thing to do, but is increasingly essential to educators' professional integrity. In many ways, physicians working in health maintenance organizations (HMOs) face challenges similar to teachers and administrators working in today's schools. These doctors are responsible for the well-being of their patients, but work within administrative structures that restrict their decision making capabilities, that are focused on saving money at least as much as on combating illness, and that do not provide the latest technology or much time and resources for professional development.

Many people are uneasy about whether conventional instruction and traditional testing are developing and assessing the types of knowledge and skills children need for their future. However, most parents and taxpayers feel that the current system worked for them and do not want to substitute something radically different unless new methods are proven to be superior.

Students are very excited when exposed to learning experiences that go beyond information assimilation and teaching-by-telling. Guided inquiry, project-based collaboration, and mentoring relationships all evoke increased learner motivation, manifested via readily observable indicators such as better attendance, higher concentration, and greater time on task. All of these not only correlate with increased educational performance, but also are in stark contrast to the attitudes parents and taxpayers formed about most of their schooling.

Documenting to communities that students care about what they are learning and are working hard to achieve complex goals is not difficult, given the ubiquity of videotape players and camcorders. Student-produced videos that show learners engaged and excited are intriguing to parents and taxpayers, who may not fully understand what is happening in the classroom, but are impressed by student behavior divergent from their own memories and likely to result in better learning outcomes. Too often, educators take little advantage of this easy way to open a dialogue about instructional improvement with the community.

In the 21st century, being a successful worker and an informed citizen will require the sophisticated knowledge delineated in the national curriculum standards, especially in the sciences and mathematics. Information technology can help students not only to learn these difficult concepts, but also to master the learning-how-to-learn skills needed to keep their capabilities current in a rapidly evolving economy.

Developing in learners the ability to use problem solving processes similar to those of experts is challenging, but provides powerful evidence that students are gaining the skills they will need to succeed in the 21st century. One of the most striking features of a classroom based on new instructional models is that learners are behaving as do teams of scientists, mathematicians, designers, or other kinds of expert problem solvers. Pupils' activities in these learning environments mirror the analytic, interpretive, creative, and expressive uses of information tools increasingly characteristic of sophisticated workplace settings.

When parents and taxpayers see students perform complex tasks and create intricate products, they are impressed by the similarity between the recent evolution of their own workplaces and the skills children are developing. Better outcomes on standardized tests. A major challenge for educational assessment is to develop methods that measure a wider range of skills than paper-and-pencil, multiple choice tests, without bogging educators down in complex, time-consuming, and potentially unreliable performance evaluations.

Research shows that students' outcomes on conventional achievement tests rise when technology-based educational innovations are implemented, but this does not occur immediately, as teachers and learners must first master these new models of pedagogy. To succeed in systemic reform, educators must prepare communities for the fact that test scores will not instantly rise and that other, complementary types of improvements less easy to report quantitatively are better short-range measures of improvement. Overall, the single most effective means of convincing parents, the business community, and taxpayers that technology-based models of teaching are superior to conventional instructional approaches is to involve them in students' education.

Certainly, new media such as Web TV are dropping in price, and almost all homes have videogames, television, and videotape players-but won't the rich always have more information devices of greater power than the poor, skewing the advantages of distributed learning and increasing inequality. From an historical perspective, innovative information technologies at first widen inequities within civilization, because initial access to the differential advantage they bring is restricted to the few who can afford the substantial expense of this increased power.

As emerging media mature, drop in price, and are widely adopted, however, the ultimate impact of information technology is to make society more egalitarian. For example, the world of universal telephone service is a more equitable environment than was the world of messenger boys and telegraph offices. The challenge for current educational policy is to minimize the period during which the gap between haves and have-nots widens, rapidly moving to a maturity of usage and an universality of access that promotes increased equity.

At present, most of society's attempts to decrease the widened inequalities that new educational technologies could create are centered on access and literacy. In schools that serve disadvantaged and at-risk populations, extra efforts are made to increase the amount of computers and communications available. Similarly, educators and learners in have-not situations are given special training to ensure that they are literate in information tools, such as web browsers.

The on-line materials and types of assistance that learners and teachers can access must reflect the needs and interests of diverse and at-risk students. Similarly, emerging graphical interfaces such as Microsoft Windows™ enhance many users' capabilities, but adversely affect learners with reduced eyesight who cannot effectively manipulate the visual features of these interfaces. The real issue in equity is empowerment-tailoring information technology to give dispossessed groups what they want.

In many ways, we live in the "Dark Ages" of schooling-restrained from making rapid advances toward increased instructional effectiveness by outmoded ideas, ritual, and tradition. For example, many people are intrigued by results from the Third International Mathematics and Science Study (TIMSS), which show the United States well behind nations such as Singapore and Japan on math and science outcomes from a globally developed achievement test.

Today, some 99% of schools are connected to the Internet, the vast majority of such connections are narrowband, with far too many computers per school connected via relatively slow links. Indeed, many children are likely to have a better online experience from their dial-up modem at home than from their 'connected' school. Those who do not have home connections will be disadvantaged: while those who do are likely become less than enthusiastic about the ICT curriculum that their school has to offer.

The process of local loop unbundling must be accelerated, and radical measures will be required to achieve this. The government should accelerate investment in the UK broadband industry through a commitment to connect all schools to broadband by 2004 at the latest, and the establishment of a network of learning hubs which will host educational content and be accessible by students and their parents, and by local community networks, via the Internet.

The New Opportunities Fund training initiative can achieve much, but in the absence of a comprehensive scheme to provide personal access to teachers, the full potential of ICT will remain untapped. The UK needs to encourage private sector investment in digital content to meet the diverse needs of the educational system and to maximise the commercial opportunities of export markets. Additionally, some of the members of the group have access to the Internet from home and were thus able to pursue further lines of enquiry and send their additional contributions to the other members of the group via e-mail outside normal school hours.

These key curricular processes and others such as measuring, controlling modelling, testing and calculating underpin much of what comprises learning, living and working in the modern world. While of course each subject in the curriculum comprises a unique and distinct set of knowledge, skills and understandings within these common curricular processes underpin every subject. Accepting that these key processes were around long before ICT, it is the ability of ICT to facilitate them, regardless of the particular subject or body of knowledge being studied, that makes it such a powerful tool for the modern educator—and even raises the question as to whether or not a subject-based curriculum remains the best approach for living, working and learning in a modern society.

However, ICT has not only supported these key curricular processes; it has facilitated a wide range of teaching and learning styles. Many of the educational activities outlined above would have been possible before the development of ICT; they have just become much more possible (and more quickly, cheaply, and conveniently) since the more general availability of ICT in schools. ICT can bring an enormous range of educational sources and resources into the classroom, support autonomous, group and whole-class teaching and bring to life topics and concepts in a way which enables teachers to teach and learners to learn.

The corporate world has long since moved away from simply buying lots of computers and then trying to network them, connect them to the Internet, set up virus protection, install Internet safety software, load application software, integrate new and existing equipment and find someone to fix it when it all goes wrong. The government and the LEAs are currently far too obsessed with the number of computers in schools rather than with the ease with which they can be supported and the effectiveness with which they can be used. Schools need to begin moving rapidly towards the concept of an ICT 'managed service' where an IT specialist company is responsible for providing an integrated service of equipment, software and support with the costs spread over 3 to 5 years.

This approach has the advantage of leaving the school free to concentrate on the effective use of the technology to improve the quality of teaching, learning and educational management. Schools have to date tended to shy away from such managed service contracts because they are perceived to be more expensive than the existing arrangements and because there is a lack of clarity, consistency and dependability in relation to school budgets. These factors significantly militate against the 3 or 5 year support contracts typically required to demonstrate the value for money advantage of a managed service approach.

For an ICT infrastructure to be sustainable not only must initial capital and running costs be affordable, but the inevitable cost of regular updating and replacement must also be accommodated. The continued dependence of schools on capital grants from central government to fund their stock of computers points to a lack of sustainability in the medium to long term.

There is an emerging debate worldwide about how schools should be provided. Even countries that are solidly committed to state funding of education are beginning to allow or encourage greater diversity in terms of who actually provides schools and learning services. Often, this involves initiatives by local parents, teachers, and community groups to take over the management of failing local-government schools, but with financial support being guaranteed by the state under some form of 'charter' agreement.

In the UK, the management of failing state schools has been contracted out to for-profit and non-profit bodies, and there is a debate about whether churches and faith groups could run state-funded schools under licence. Other countries, such as the Netherlands and Denmark, have lived with state funding but diverse provision for many years. Not only does such diversity give choice to parents; it encourages innovation and customer-focus, and bids up standards as schools strive to win the support of more parents and so increase their share of the state's funding.

Online curriculum content and the other opportunities opened up by ICT are, we believe, other areas where the benefits of diversity will be clear. A sector which is moving so quickly, and which exists precisely in order to generate new ideas and new ways of working, is ill-suited to being managed and regulated by government-style institutions, which are inevitably rather bureaucratic and slow-moving. Rather, it should be regulated through the much more dynamic process of customer choice. But for that system to work, customers must possess the actual power to exercise their choices.

The availability of these e-credits (which could only be spent on digital courses and resources) would provide a stimulus for schools, educational publishers and others to do what a few pioneers have already done - to develop online curricula that could be purchased and used by other educational establishments or indeed individual learners. In the e-credit world, ICT funding would increasingly follow the learner. A wide range of e-credit courses could be developed and pupils would be entitled to use their credits to pursue them. Allowing pupils to take their ecredits elsewhere will increase diversity, choice and competition, and push up standards.

Some e-courses may involve home-based learning (properly monitored and supported), while others would be based almost entirely at a local school. Such courses might well provide a mix of interactive multimedia materials, text and video conferencing resources and access to relevant experts. This opens up the possibility of students being able to follow courses from a range of educational providers, whilst still 'attending' the same school.

The e-credit could also change the economics of what is a viable school - in particularly, creating the opportunity for smaller, community-based learning institutions to offer a broader range of professionally-constructed courses, while they focus on improved tutorial support and/or pastoral care. And by mitigating physical capacity constraints, good schools that employ online learning strategies could continue to expand. The e-credit could enhance the ability of a school to supplement (or replace) the work of an under-performing department, by buying in courses from other institutions.

Once e-credits have been introduced via the pump priming funding mentioned earlier, they should become self funding as schools move resources from more traditional areas. In the medium term, the evidence base for the impact of ICT on education costs and outcomes, and for the opportunities that it creates, will become clear and will inform future investment decisions. Widespread access to ICT facilities would enable much of the bureaucratic burden on teachers and schools to be removed. There are virtually no aspects of the teacher's workload which could not be improved through such access.

Attendance recording, curriculum planning, assessment and reporting, and lesson preparation are but a few of the opportunities. The provision of educational broadband would facilitate the development of a range of competing educational support services, which would have the advantage of reducing the administrative burden on teachers. Such educational support services would encompass a wide range of personal development and management functions and would go much further than many initiatives to date.

Online Curriculum

In more recent times the role of ICT has been seen as much more crosscurricular, a facilitating and enhancing agent rather than one specifically structured around individual subjects. The cross-curricular approach has much to commend it, principally that it provides a meaningful context in which ICT capability could be developed and through which it could contribute to the development of higher-order thinking skills. A recent publication by the OECD suggests that this failure to embed ICT into existing practice is a result of the 'closed' nature of the school curriculum and that ICT will only become truly effective after a 'radical and systemic change' to the nature of schools.

Unfortunately, the government's Curriculum Online proposals anticipate much less radical implications arising from the use of ICT in schools. It is almost apologetic about the fundamental nature of the contribution of ICT when it states: 'We recognise very clearly that what we are proposing here is not a replacement for traditional and tried teaching methods, but should be integrated with them. New forms of accessing information, great works of art, sources of knowledge and imaginative ways of presenting traditional facts are complementary to, rather than a replacement for, the critical core skills on which we have placed such emphasis.' This potential lack of vision in respect of the implications of the digital curriculum was challenged in the response of the General Teaching Council when it responded diplomatically:

'The Curriculum Online consultation paper articulates a vision of a 'digital education', which complements 'traditional teaching methods' in raising standards. ... Nevertheless the Council considers the dichotomy between teaching and learning enabled and shaped by digital resources and that construed as 'traditional' presented in the vision for Curriculum Online to be an artificial one.

Teachers need opportunities for reflective practice to embed innovation and change. If UK education is to benefit fully from the contribution which ICT can make to improving standards, it needs to remember the key lesson learned from the introduction of new technology into business: don't just computerise existing practice: change the practice to fully exploit the new opportunity. That points to the need to consider the opportunity for fundamental curriculum reform. It is already clear that in the longer term the key contribution that ICT can make to such reform is its ability to:

— motivate pupils;
— encourage autonomous learning;
— facilitate differentiated learning experiences;
— allow the curriculum to be tailored to the needs of individual pupils;
— broaden the range of sources and resources available;
— provide improved feedback on learning outcomes.

In a world where, increasingly, learning can take place and any time and in any place we need to consider issues such as:

— the hours during which schools open;
— the role of teachers;
— the balance between number of teachers and other support professionals;
— the organisation of learning groups;
— the interaction with the home; and
— pastoral care arrangements.

These changes point to a dramatically improved opportunity to put the needs of the individual learner at the heart of or education system, and point to opportunities for change in the way schools operate.

8

Policies and Programmes in Curriculum Reforms

The rate of return to schooling is an important parameter in labour economics and having a good estimate is clearly important for public policy as well as for individuals. In recent years considerable research effort has been invested in refining the estimation techniques used to estimate this parameter. Recent research on the returns to schooling (along with other areas of labor research such as the impact of training) has drawn analogies with 'treatment' and 'control' group concepts in the medical/psychology literature.

Since random assignment of schooling is not possible, the literature on returns to schooling is increasingly focused on finding natural experiments that exogenously assign individuals to different treatments, thus creating 'natural' variation in data. For example Angrist and Krueger explore how an individual's season of birth may imply that some students reach school leaving age after fewer months of compulsory education than others, allowing for the creation of suitable instruments to exploit in an Instrumental Variables (IV) approach.

Harmon and Walker use the change in compulsory schooling law, which raised the minimum schooling age in Britain to generate an exogenous change in education. In both of these approaches the key variable will affect the education decisions of a subset of the population, those who leave school as soon as they can, so one interpretation of these results is that the IV estimates identify the rate of return to the marginal or "treated" group only.

Technology is an important tool in improving higher education, but it is not the short-term solution to lowering the costs of such education. One approach is performancebased reform. In 1959 only 20 percent of all prime-age jobs required at least some college; by 1997 the proportion was 56 percent. By 1998 more than 80 percent of managers and professionals had at least some college education, up from 59 percent 25 years earlier. Those in high-technology jobs followed a similar pattern, while the proportion of college-trained workers in education and health care started high and climbed even higher.

The need for postsecondary education has increased substantially even for occupations not usually associated with book learning. The share of clerical workers with some college education has more than doubled, from 25 percent to 54 percent since 1973, while the share of skilled blue-collar workers with some college education has increased from 17 percent to 28 percent.This progression has been neither even nor universal, however. Disparities persist along economic and racial lines. Nearly 80 percent of high school graduates from high-income families went directly to college in 1997, while only half the high school graduates from low-income families did so.

The low-income population remains disproportionately minority, and this is also where the educational fault line lies. Among young adults ages 25 to 29 in 1999, white high school graduates were more than twice as likely to have earned a bachelor's degree than high school graduates who were African American or Hispanic. The proportion of African American and Hispanic high school graduates enrolled in college has been rising but still .lags behind. While 46 percent of college-age white high school graduates were enrolled in college in 1997, the proportions were 39 percent for African Americans and 36 percent for Hispanics.These percentages are encouraging because they represent a narrowing of the education gap.

Closing the racial and ethnic education gap not only would advance individual opportunity, but also would enhance the nation's wealth. For example, if we could equalize majority and minority college-level attainment, we would reduce the share of Hispanic families with officially determined "inadequate incomes" from 41 percent to 21 percent and that of African American families from 33 percent to 24 percent.Moreover, the benefits would extend far beyond minority families. The increase in human capital would also add more than $230 billion to the nation's income, providing an additional $80 billion in new tax revenues.Increased growth in state wealth would be $73 billion in California, $44 billion in Texas, and $22 billion in New York, and it would also spread broadly among most states.

College-level talent is a basic resource in growing the knowledge economy. Historically, increases in education have driven about 25 percent of the growth in the gross domestic product. With high school graduation rates moving toward 90 percent, future educational contributions to overall growth will have to come from increasing participation in prekindergarten development and increased years of postsecondary education. In addition, the rapid increase in the earnings of college graduates relative to the earnings of high school graduates through the mid-1990s is clear evidence of a shortage of college-educated workers and an oversupply of high school-educated workers.

Demography is destiny in postsecondary education. Research shows that both minority and majority students on diverse campuses learn problem-solving, leadership, and other critical work skills better than students on campuses with more homogeneous student bodies. Similar benefits would accrue as students enter the workforce. There is increasing evidence that diverse work teams help institutions interact successfully with a more varied market at home and abroad; discourage "groupthink;" and encourage learning, creativity, and flexibility on the job.

In today's global economy, these competencies are important competitive assets. Celebrations are Premature. The large numbers of prospective minority college students may mask continued education gaps. Even with an additional 600,000 African Americans and Hispanics on campuses, Hispanic 18- to 24-year-olds are expected to be underrepresented in college by 8 percentage points and African Americans by 3 percentage points. If a smaller share of a larger pool of minority youth takes college admissions exams and enrolls in college, admission test scores and college performance ratings are likely to improve even as equal opportunity suffers.

Furthermore, preparing all students for college will require major investments to offer prekindergarten education and to reform elementary and secondary education. It may be tempting to meet some of those needs by diverting crucial public dollars from higher education. In addition, the overall surge in college-age youths will tax the ability of higher education institutions to meet the increased demand. Many institutions may turn to technology as an answer, but technology is expensive and is not likely to increase efficiency in time to reduce costs for these prospective students.

All of these factors combine to encourage tuition increases just when the opposite-more affordable higher education-is what is needed to extend access. Governors must respond to the challenges of meeting increased demand and closing persistent educational gaps. Social capital is the collateral necessary for human capital development.

A significant barrier to postsecondary education among nontraditional students as well as low-income and minority high school graduates is that they are not aware of the many college opportunities open to them nor do they know how to apply for these benefits. Therefore, expanded counseling and recruitment efforts would likely have very large payoffs. For example, research conducted by the National Center for Education Statistics showed that Hispanic high school graduates who are qualified for college are less likely to attend college than similarly qualified white graduates.

However, the research showed no difference in postsecondary entry between white high school graduates and Hispanic graduates who take the necessary steps to get into a four -year college, such as taking the College Board test and applying to college.This suggests that minority families may be losing out on a college education because they do not know the admission process. Informational and counseling remedies, which are not very expensive, could go a long way to bolster Hispanic participation in higher education.

Low-income and minority students depend heavily on student assistance, but aid has not kept pace with college costs. While 17 percent of white undergraduates currently receive federal need-based aid, 38 percent of African American and 36 percent of Hispanic undergraduates do so.Yet the real value of needbased student aid has fallen far behind the increase in college costs and even farther behind the amounts necessary to close the gap between low-income families' needs and college costs.

We know that low-income student enrollments are more sensitive to increases in college costs than middle- and upper-income enrollments. One study, for example, shows that for every $1,000 annual increase in the price tag at a community college, enrollments decline by 6 percent.Even if low-income and minority students have access to some form of postsecondary education, the overwhelming majority is shut out of the most selective four-year colleges. Among students at four-year colleges whose family income places them in the lowest quintile, only 8 percent attend the 120 most selective colleges. Only 34 percent of African American students and 25 percent of Hispanic students attend the most selective 1,000 four -year colleges.

More than half of Hispanic students attend community colleges.Changes in student aid policy have hindered access to postsecondary education for low-income and minority students. Federal financial aid has shifted toward middle-income students since Congress adopted the Middle Income Student Assistance Act during President Jimmy Carter's tenure. Grants are more helpful to low-income students, while loans favor middle-income families. Yet loans have become the dominant form of aid, currently amounting to more than five times the value of grants. Meanwhile, the recent shift to tax-based aid in the form of credits and deductions also favors higher-income families that fill out the long form of income tax returns. At the same time, state and institutional aid programs have switched to merit-based aid that is targeted to middle-income families.

The need to increase access to higher education will run head-on into an inevitable budget crunch for all of education. As human capital emerges as the critical ingredient in economic growth in the knowledge economy, the pressure to spend money on all facets of education will become relentless. Governors will confront urgent demands for spending scarce public dollars on crucial priorities all along an expanded education pipeline-to make prekindergarten universal, to institute standards-based reform of elementary and secondary education, and to increase the capacity of postsecondary education institutions to accommodate all potential students.

Universal prekindergarten, for example, could cost as much as $40 billion. The additional 1.6 million postsecondary students anticipated by 2015 could cost higher education $19 billion. States, which currently pick up 35 percent of the postsecondary education bill, would have to come up with more than $6 billion at a time when they have been reducing their share of higher education spending.Ironically, in the competition for state dollars among the education sectors, governors may find it harder to justify expenditures for higher education than for prekindergarten and elementary and secondary education.

Postsecondary education may become a victim of its own success and structure. If this happens, the real victims would be those who are thus denied access to higher education and the larger society that will be denied the intellectual and economic benefits of their contributions. Higher education is viewed as more successful and less in need of help than other parts of the education system.

Unlike elementary and secondary education, higher education is a market-based system responsive to market changes. Because it is less regulated than the elementary and secondary education sectors, higher education can adapt to cost realities more easily. The results of those adaptations are diffused through a decentralized higher education system and thus more difficult to discern. But that does not mean that society will not feel the impact of those adaptations.

Perhaps most important, higher education also has the ability to help pay for itself simply by raising tuition. However, the decision to raise college tuition and fees should not be taken lightly. It is true that college is still a very good deal, even though rising college costs has increasingly alarmed Americans. College degrees are still worth anywhere from eight to ten times their cost. That calculation may be a difficult one for median-income families, however. They have witnessed a doubling of college costs since the 1970s, while their own incomes have gone up by less than 25 percent.

A decision to make colleges and universities try to pay for increasing costs by raising tuition and fees could prove counterproductive. Higher tuition will discourage enrollments, especially among low-income and minority students, the bulk of the potential new student population. Moreover, tight budgets will discourage the maintenance of quality improvements already in place and delay new investments in educational quality. Thus, the market response to this decision could be a classic case of market failure for higher education.

Reengineering and technology will not solve the short-term cost problems. Technology cannot come to the rescue in time to serve the flood of new students who began arriving on college campuses in 1997. Ultimately, the reengineering of higher education into transparent institutional learning networks will make college cheaper, faster, and better for individual students, but it is less certain that efficiency improvements can increase faster than the overall demand for access. Nor is it likely that technology will save us by creating "virtual universities" for new students.

Most people are not ready to get their education from a computer screen; they still want to get it in a college setting in which they interact with real professors and flesh-and-blood fellow students. In general, experience with technology in other service industries shows that technology adds value more than it reduces cost. It can reduce costs eventually, but the initial investments are expensive. And the most powerful longterm effects are not to reduce costs but to provide new kinds of added value in the form of quality, variety, customization, convenience, speed, and novelty.

Performance-based reform can deliver higher education cheaper, faster and better. Governors are going to feel relentless pressure to find scarce resources to meet the growing economic need for postsecondary education. Rather than raising tuition or raising taxes, the most effective approach will be seeking performance-based reform. The introduction of performance standards and their alignment with assessments, curricula, and teacher preparation is already well underway in elementary and secondary education.

Performance standards have grown steadily for vocationally oriented proprietary schools and community colleges. They are poised to spread to four-year colleges and graduate academic and professional programs. There is an important caveat in the adoption of performance-based standards by institutions of higher education, however. Colleges and universities do more than simply prepare students for jobs. They also perform academic and cultural roles that are critical in a participatory political system and an indiv idualistic culture. These missions must be factored into the higher education equation. At the same time, however, higher education cannot fulfill its cultural and academic missions without paying attention to its economic role.

Solutions for Educational Improvement

If any educational reform is likely to exacerbate social exclusion, to leave disadvantaged groups out of the improvement process, then it cannot be tolerated. Conversely, any educational reform that could be seen to be promoting social inclusion is going to be more desirable than one that doesn't, other things being equal. Part of promoting equity in this way, of course, means that educational standards must be raised in areas where they are currently too low. To achieve opportunity for all, and to raise educational standards, the government says that its reforms must promote 'diversity' and 'autonomy'.

Through diversity, the government wants to encourage 'all schools to build a distinct ethos and centre of excellence'. And diversity is valued for three distinct reasons:

— Because young people have different needs and ambitions, and schools must reflect these: schools should 'cater significantly better for the diverse requirements and aspirations of today's young people'. Schools must 'develop the talents of each individual pupil to the full'.

— Parents, too, may have different preferences for their children. Through diversity schools can be 'better able to reflect parental preferences'.

— Diversity for both young people and parents means greater choice. Indeed, one of the four 'key objectives' that the prime minister laid out on 16th July 2001 for reform of the public services, including education, was the need for 'greater consumer choice'.

Autonomy and diversity, then, are based on the underlying core values of greater freedom, greater innovation and greater choice. There are 'market approaches' found throughout the world, aimed at addressing precisely the kind of problems raised above. These include public funding of private schools; privatisation of state schools; voucher schemes; tax credit schemes; public-private partnerships and contracting out to the private sector. Such approaches, based on global experience, can usefully be classified into three ideal types:

— Alternative funding

— Alternative schools

— Alternative providers

An education voucher is a coupon or a cheque provided by government to parents, for them to spend with an education provider of their choice. These can be universal or targeted - that is, for all children, or for particularly targeted groups. The only two countries with universal vouchers are Sweden and Chile, though there are several targeted schemes in countries as diverse as the USA, Bangladesh, New Zealand and Columbia. The Swedish voucher scheme is probably the most radical market reform in existence anywhere in the world.

The Swedish reforms occurred in 1992, when municipalities were obliged to give 85% of the calculated average cost per student in the municipal schools to any school of parent choice - for all students, not just some targeted groups. Enrolment rules were also opened within the public sector, with money following the pupils into public-sector schools in other municipalities. The figure of 85% was calculated so as to give equal funding to the independent schools, with the other 15% accounting for overhead and administration of the municipalities.

Significantly, as long as schools fulfil certain basic requirements, any kind of school is eligible, from religious schools to schools run by for-profit corporations. This is different from the situation in Denmark and the Netherlands, where private schools have had a long tradition of receiving public funding, but only particular kinds of parent-controlled, not-for-profit schools are allowed to receive public funds. A rapid growth of independent schools has been experienced since the reforms were introduced, although this differs between municipalities.

Municipalities are allowed to say whether they consider the establishment of a new independent school would be harmful to existing schools, and their views must be taken into account by the National Agency for

Education (NAE). Importantly, however, they have no veto on this, and must, by law, finance any independent school that has been approved by the NAE, which indeed has approved schools against the municipality's will.

In America there are various schemes of specifically targeted vouchers, most famously those in Milwaukee and Cleveland. Milwaukee's publicly funded voucher scheme - the Milwaukee Parent Choice Program (MPCP) - was introduced in 1990, specifically targeting low-income families to allow them to attend registered private schools. The voucher's value is set at the per-student subsidy rate provided to the government schools by the state. Parents qualify for a voucher only if their family income is no more than 1.75 times the official poverty level.

In 1995 the programme was expanded, allowing around 15,000 students to participate. In 1998 the growth of the programme burgeoned when the Wisconsin Supreme Court ruled that religious schools could participate in the programme, a decision endorsed by the US Supreme Court in 2002. The Cleveland voucher programme is similar, having been enacted in 1995 with legislation modelled on the Milwaukee system.

Religious schools could participate in the programme right from the start, and children who were currently attending private schools could apply for the vouchers. Families with incomes below the poverty line received 90% of tuition fees and those above the cut off point 75% of the tuition fees. In its first year, 1996, the programme was limited to 2,000 students and for children who were enrolled in kindergarten to grade 3. By the end of 1996 this target had been met -with around 2,000 children receiving vouchers, enrolled in the 55 private schools operating in the Cleveland voucher scheme.

An alternative 'targeted voucher' approach has been tried in Florida, the Florida A+ Plan for Education, which targets failure of state schools, rather than poverty. The programme provides vouchers when a government school is rated a grade F twice in a period of four years. The grade is determined by the performance of students taking the Florida Comprehensive Assessment Tests (FCAT) in maths, reading, and writing. The A+ Education Plan was introduced in Florida in June 1999 and became the first statewide voucher programme to be implemented in the USA.

The idea is that schools will improve their performance owing to the fear of being shamed into closing or loosing students and revenue. The value of the voucher received by parents in Florida has a maximum limit of $4,000 and this may be spent in any independent secular, religious or government school.

Finally, to dispel once and for all the notion that targeted voucher schemes have anything to do with the perpetuation of privilege, we can see that targeted vouchers have been used in developing countries specifically to target some of the most disadvantaged people on the planet. In Colombia, a targeted voucher system was introduced in 1992, aimed at providing wider access to private education for poor students, inspired by the realisation that there was a shortage of places offered by state secondary schools. The proposal allowed poor children to benefit from private school provision, moving out of the overcrowded public sector.

Central government shares the cost of the vouchers with the local governments participating in the scheme, although the financial burden is not equally distributed between them - 80% of the cost is financed by central government with the remaining 20% being taken up by the municipalities. Importantly, the private schools taking part offer an educational service that had been estimated to be of comparable quality to that found in government schools; and yet the typical cost of sending a pupil to private school, via the voucher scheme, is around two-thirds of the per-pupil cost of sending him or her to a government school.

After two years, the programme served 90,807 low-income students in a total of 1,789 schools. By 1997 more than 100,000 students from very low-income families had received subsidies through the programme. Similarly, in 1982 in Bangladesh, the Female Secondary Education Scholarship Project piloted a targeted voucher scheme. This programme was aimed at girls from low-income families who otherwise would not have been able to obtain a secondary school education; this programme is therefore gender specific. Girls who receive the scholarships are able to attend secondary school at half the tuition cost for the first three grades of the school. Before the scheme was introduced, in areas participating in the project, female enrolment in secondary education hovered at around 27%; by 1987, this figure had risen to almost 44%.

The second form of alternative funding is the educational tax credit, which can take one of three main forms:

— Non-refundable tax credits are where a family pays for its child's education in private school, and then has this cost subtracted from its annual tax payment. § Refundable tax credits are where a sum more than one's tax burden can be claimed, so those who pay little or no tax receive additional funds.

— Tax credits may also be used to allow businesses or philanthropically-minded individuals to fund a disadvantaged child's private education, and for the business or individual to count this contribution against their tax liability.

Educational Tax Credits

The first US states to introduce tax credits were Minnesota and Arizona in 1997, followed by Iowa in 1998, Illinois in 1999 and Pennsylvania in 2001. In Pennsylvania corporations can receive tax credits to the amount of 75% of their contributions. In Minnesota, the scheme allows a $1,000 tax credit per student for families with incomes up to $37,500. These tax credits can be used for private tutoring, textbooks, school transport, computers and instructional materials, but not for school fees.

Families with incomes above this level receive a tax deduction of up to $2,500 for private school fees, as well as the other expenses that are covered under the tax credit. In all of the states apart from Minnesota and Arizona, tax credits can be set against tuition costs. All states allow the claim to be made against materials and other forms of schooling, apart from Arizona. The majority of the tax credit schemes are not means tested, although the maximum value of the tax credit is prescribed in each state.

In Arizona taxpayers receive a dollar-for-dollar tax credit when they donate to scholarship organisations providing support for students who attend or wish to attend private school. Taxpayers can make individual donation of up to $500 per year, and a married couple $625 per year. This has led, between 1998-2000, to donations of approximately $32 million generated by these educational tax credits, funding 19,000 scholarships. The Canadian province of Ontario is also introducing a tax credit scheme. The scheme will allow a qualifying taxpayer to claim a tax credit of a certain percentage of eligible tuition fees paid to an eligible independent school. Starting in 2002 taxpayers can claim 10% of fees, rising 10% each year until 50% can be claimed in 2006.

Tax relief of various shapes and sizes are also common in Europe too. In over half of the countries in the European Union, tax relief is available to cover educational expenses. In Germany, for instance, parents who send their children to (subsidised) private schools are eligible for certain allowances against tax including:

— support for a child at boarding school

— 30% of the cost of all school fees

— transport costs.

Tax relief is also available for books, materials and transport costs in France, Greece, Luxembourg, Belgium, Spain, Italy, Portugal and the Netherlands.

Public Funding of Private Schools

Another market approach to supporting choice, freedom and autonomy in education is through public funding of private schools. This is a model in common currency across the world, in Europe, America and other countries such as Hong Kong. Interestingly, the British government is also keen to emphasise diversity of provision in state education. It has created its own kind of state-subsidised private school, the 'City Academies' - now 'Academies' - that allow for the creation of new, state-of-the-art independent schools that will get their per capita pupil funding from the state, and which will need private funding for their capital construction.

However, a global perspective shows that this type of school is rather out of keeping with developments elsewhere. City Academies are huge, capital-rich projects that are unlikely to be accessible to many promoters. In most of Europe and in America, by contrast, the view is that 'small is beautiful, and grassroots organisations are empowered to open new schools and explore new methods.

It sometimes seems the accepted wisdom here is that private-sector involvement in education is very much an Anglo-Saxon obsession, confined to those greedy Americans and their British lackeys; and that only in rotten Britain do we have this divisive trend, different from our communitarian neighbours. In fact, widespread private education -and even more remarkably, widespread government support of private education - is commonplace throughout the European Union.

The British government seems to want to have its cake and eat it - to regulate private education as heavily as other European countries, while at the same time offering no financial support. The important point is that the principle of support of private education is well established across mainland Europe. Supporting market approaches to education does not put Britain out of step in Europe. It is crucial to emphasise this.

In Netherland, a scheme ensuring freedom of parental choice in education has been in operation for almost 100 years, enshrined in the constitution of 1917. Altogether about 70% of children attend private schools - the majority of which are church schools, with a total of 7% at non-religious private schools. Schools include Montessori and

Steiner, together with Jewish, Islamic, Hindu and humanist schools. There is ease of entry for new suppliers. Any group of parents or other interested parties can make application to the Ministry of Education, Culture and Science to establish a new school.

All government and private grant aided schools are guaranteed the same financial support. Interestingly, although private schools are not allowed to charge top-up fees, they are allowed to receive contributions from parents to purchase teaching materials, fund extra-curricular activities, employ additional staff or pay teachers a supplement to their regular salaries. These 'fees' range from $100 to $200 per year at most primary schools, higher at secondary schools.

Denmark shares with the Netherlands the key feature that there is a Constitutional right for parents to set up their own schools and receive state funding. Currently, about 12% of primary and lower-secondary students are in the private sector, and 5% of upper secondary students. 21% of schools at the primary and lower-secondary level are in the private sector. Since the Free School Act of 1855, parents and organisations have been able to set up their own schools.

Any private organisation or group of adults or parents can set up a private school for children between 6 and 18 years of age. To receive government funding, the minimum size for a primary or lower secondary private school is only 28 pupils after three years: with at least 12 pupils enrolled in the first year, 20 in the second year and from then on, 28 pupils. All approved private schools are entitled to receive state subsidies covering about 80% of their operational expenditure on the basis of the number of pupils enrolled at the individual school in a given year, plus a capital allowance, and other special grants. On top of these grants, parents pay a moderate fee - something long accepted in Denmark as an important principle of family responsibility.

In Germany private education is expanding at a remarkable rate. Growth is fastest in the east German Länder, where private schools, first allowed only in 1990, had grown to some 154 by 1998. In the west German Länder, growth of around 14% was experienced between 1992 and 1998. At the Gymnasium, (lower and upper secondary school), 10.3% of pupils are in the private sector, and there are 11.3% of schools in the private sector at this level. For Realschule, the level is 7.1% of pupils; special schools are 16.4% in the private sector. So, at certain levels of schooling, private education in Germany is significantly higher than in the UK. In terms of financing, the Land governments are required to ensure private schools' existence under constitutional entitlements.

In practice, all of the Länder provide subsidies to private schools, provided that they are non-profit bodies. Such financial support includes subsidies for staffing costs, and is usually a lump sum comparable to that in the state schools. In addition, there are subsidies to cover construction costs, textbooks and teachers' pension funds. Importantly, private schools are allowed to charge fees to cover their extra costs. They are also not required to follow the same timetables or curricula as public sector schools, and are also free to choose their textbooks. They are free to promote religious or philosophical views, and use teaching methods of their own choice.

Moreover, private schools have complete freedom to hire and fire teaching staff, and inspection is fairly minimal. In Hong Kong an interesting form of state subsidy has emerged, reinforced and extended since the colony reverted to China. Here, fee-paying school places are provided for about 85% of the 15-year-old cohort. Importantly, publicly funded private schools are permitted to charge fees. And to counteract the argument that the introduction of school fees will exclude children from low-income families, the Hong Kong government introduced a Fee Remission Policy. This is designed to channel a percentage of funds collected from fees into subsidised places to the poor.

While for-profit companies are allowed to operate schools, the majority of publicly funded schools in Hong Kong are owned and managed by churches, trusts and private organisations. Private schools that receive public funds are defined as Aided Schools and receive specific grants from the Department of Education for staff costs and all operating expenses. Grants that cover operating costs are calculated depending on the number of classes, students and subjects taught. Perhaps the best known (in Britain) kind of public subsidy of private schools are the charter schools in the USA.

Charter schools are free from direct administrative government control and are under fewer regulatory constraints than state schools. They must, however, meet the performance standards set by their charter. This freedom allows charter schools to have more control over their curriculum, hours of operation, the staff they employ, budget and internal organisation, and schedule. The funding they receive is based upon the number of pupils in attendance - so fewer pupils means less funding. The concept was first introduced in 1991, in Minnesota, and by January 2000, there was charter legislation in 36 states, plus the District of Columbia, with over 500,000 students enrolled in charter schools. During the 2000-01 school year there were 2,069 charter schools operating in America.

Charter schools can be converted state schools, converted private schools, or new schools. In fact, about 70% of charter schools are brand-new schools. Charter schools are not allowed to charge tuition fees in any state, although it is possible to invite voluntary contributions from parents for building projects. In general, too, charter schools can - and do - go bankrupt: they are not protected by the state from this happening, and will do so if they have not been able to attract sufficient students, or have poorly managed their budgets. In all states too, if there is excess demand for places - as there is in some 70% of charter schools -places are allocated by 'equitable means' such as a lottery. Three types of organisation are attracted to the charter school market:

— Charities seeking to promote a particular way of life, such as Heritage Academies promoting 'American values and civic pride'.

— Charities promoting improved education for disadvantaged or ignored groups.

— For-profit companies, which are allowed to manage charter schools in 21 of the 36 states - including Arizona, Massachusetts and Michigan.

The final type of alternative delivery mechanism is to allow 'alternative providers', forprofit education companies, to bring the disciplines of the private sector to the state education sector. Sometimes, alternative providers arise naturally in response to market reforms - in Sweden, for example, where the rise of for-profit education companies followed the wide availability of vouchers. In other places, they arise through for-profit companies themselves seeing the opportunity and creating the mechanisms to contract with local education authorities to manage state schools.

Explore Learning

In UK, a for-profit education company, Explore Learning, run by Bill Mills, a 35-year old educational entrepreneur, is running a learning centre, and aiming to roll out the business model to supermarkets across the country. The centre offers supplementary learning to six to 13-year olds, to help them improve in mathematics, English, science and ICT. The key to the attractiveness of the project is that it uses innovative educational software, including Success Maker, which adjusts to the achievement level of the child, rather than assuming the child has to progress at the same level as a mixed-ability class. The first classroom - in space rented from the supermarket chain - has around 24 workstations that are run by a rotating team of young graduates, who work with children in groups of about six, are paid at teaching levels, but are not necessarily qualified as teachers.

The key is that they must be enthused with a love of learning and want to share this with children. Significantly, the centre costs about £50 per month, for a maximum of 10 hours per student. So when mum and dad are shopping, the child can spend an hour in the learning centres. Those who are doing well at school are challenged to extend their skills and knowledge. Most importantly, those who find school difficult are encouraged to focus on where their difficulties lie, being given help that is often singularly lacking at school.

Importantly, these high quality educational opportunities, with one to one learning, are offered for only about £5 per hour. This makes it very competitive with the costs of what is offered in state schools. Market approaches are being used across the world, in Europe and America and elsewhere. There are three principles are:

— Raising standards in education.

— Enhancing opportunity for all.

— Promoting the virtues of choice, diversity and innovation in education.

In fact, the evidence from around the world shows that market approaches satisfy all three of these principles. Indeed, on the basis of this evidence, we can say that:

— Market approaches raise standards in education, better than non-market approaches and often at a lower cost.

— Market approaches are more equitable, helping extend access and opportunity to the most disadvantaged in society, better than non-market alternatives.

— Market approaches ensure choice, diversity, and innovation, as well as increased investment, in education, better than non-market approaches.

Perhaps the most dramatic results show how competition from the private sector helps improve standards in state schools. This effect has been demonstrated whether one looks at universal vouchers, targeted vouchers, charter schools or publicly-funded private schools.

— In the universal voucher system of Sweden, research has found that competition from independent schools improves test results and final grades in the state schools. The higher the proportion of students in private schools, when controlled for the normal factors, the higher the grades in the state schools.

— The Florida A+ Plan, the voucher scheme that targets failing state schools, has succeeded in stimulating school improvement in state schools. As one commentator put it, the A+ Plan instilled in the state schools 'a sense of urgency and zeal for reform not seen in the past when a school's failure was rewarded only with the money that reinforced failure'. Research has shown that schools awarded an F grade one year - meaning that they would lose pupils through the voucher scheme if they failed a second year - were achieving the largest improvement gains in the state.

— From Milwaukee, too, there is some evidence of government schools being stimulated into improvement. As one commentator put it: the state system 'realises that it can no longer take parents for granted'.

— Finally, Charter schools have also been shown to have a similar impact.

One study found that, when schools and school districts were faced with competition from charter schools, they responded with changes in district and schoollevel behaviour, in terms of the promotion of pedagogical experimentation, increasing technology in the school, introducing new programmes, supporting teacher efforts to upgrade curriculum, and introducing in-service training. They found that the greatest effects were in the 'more troubled school districts', and that the changes were more marked when the competition was higher. The effects were modest in size - but then the changes had only been running for three years.

In some countries, improvements are obtained at a lower per capita cost than is found in the state sector. In Denmark, for instance, independent schools operate at a per pupil cost that is roughly 90-96% of the per pupil cost in public schools, although they deliver higher achievement. Nor are private schools in Britain as costly than their much lower pupil:staff ratios might suggest. Worldwide, competition seems to have the effect of reducing the costs of education in the private sector - even though independent schools typically are much smaller and so cannot have economies of scale.

Market approaches that have been tried around the world have been found to have a very beneficial impact on the most disadvantaged of communities. Research on the universal voucher system in Sweden has shown that the share of students attending private schools is larger, the worst performing are the state schools. In other words, there is no evidence that 'independent schools are more likely to be established in municipalities with "easy customers"', but rather that they are established often to serve disadvantaged young people. Moreover, there is no evidence that 'low-achievers are adversely affected by increased competition from independent schools'.

All the alternative approaches above increase parental and student choice, and promote diversity. Parents value this choice and have greater satisfaction with the schools that are chosen. There is also evidence to show such schools improving innovation and raising increased investment in the state sector. Surveys from the Danish Ministry of Finance show parents with children in independent schools are, on average, more satisfied with their schools than parents in public schools: 86% of parents are satisfied or very satisfied with their school. And comparing parent satisfaction on issues such as teacher skills and parent influence on schools, private school parents are more satisfied on almost all issues than public school parents.

Bibliography

Altbach PG, "The dilemma of change in Indian higher education", *Higher Education*. 26: 3-20, 1999.

Balan J, "Governance and finance of national universities in Argentina: current proposals for change", *Higher Education*, 25: 45-59, 1993

Ball C and Eggins H (eds), "Higher Education into the 1990s", Milton Keynes: SRHE and Open University Press, 1989

Barrow CW, "The strategy of selective excellence: redesigning higher education for global competition in a post-industrial society", *Higher Education*. 41: 447-469.

Breier M (ed) "Curriculum Restructuring in Higher Education in Post-Apartheid South Africa", Pretoria: CSD, 2001

Chitnis, S, "Gearing a colonial system of education to take independent India towards development", *Higher Education*, 26: 21-41, 1993

Daniel J, "The challenge of mass higher education", *Studies in Higher Education*, 18(2): 197-203, 1993.

Eggins H (ed), "Restructuring Higher Education. Milton Keynes: SRHE and Open University Press, 1988.

Ensor P, "Axes of Choice in Curriculum Planning: A Commentary on the Grahamstown Seminar", In: Chet: The New Qualifications Framework for Higher Education: a second reader. Pretoria: Chet, 1999.

Ganderton PS, "Concepts of globalisation and their impact upon curriculum policy-making: rhetoric and reality", *a study of*

Australian reform. International Journal of Educational Development. 16(4): 393-405, 1996.

Green A, "Education and globalization in Europe and East Asia: convergent and divergent trends", *Journal of Education Policy*. 14(1): 55-71, 1999.

Govinden D, "Perspectives in Education Special issue; Higher Education, globalisation and the Third World state". 18(3), 2000

Jansen J and Christie P (eds), "Changing Curriculum: Studies on Outcomes-based education in South Africa", Cape Town: Juta, 1999.

Lattuca LR and Stark JS, "Will disciplinary perspectives impede curricula reform", *Journal of Higher Education*. 65(4): 401-426, 1994

Index